KEEPING US IN THE DARK

KEEPING US IN THE DARK

CENSORSHIP AND FREEDOM OF INFORMATION IN IRELAND

Brendan Ryan

GILL & MACMILLAN

Gill & Macmillan Ltd
Goldenbridge
Dublin 8
with associated companies throughout the world

© Brendan Ryan 1995
0 7171 2232 8
Index compiled by
Helen Litton
Design and print origination by
O'K Graphic Design, Dublin
Printed by
ColourBooks Ltd, Dublin

A catalogue record for this book is available from the British Library.

1 3 5 4 2

For Clare, Sinéad, Eilis, and Conall

CONTENTS

• •

Acknowledgments   ix
1. Introduction   1

Part 1: *We Know They Know but Still They Won't Tell Us*
2. How They Form Us: Educating in Ignorance   13
3. For Our Own Good   24
4. The Air that We Breathe   35
5. Keeping Us Safe   48
6. Keeping the Poor in Their Place   59
7. Trust Me, I Know What I'm Doing   71
8. Rich, Powerful, Secret, and Greedy   79

Part 2: *What They Know About Us*
9. The Data Protection Act   92
10. From the Cradle to the Grave   102

Part 3: *Reclaiming Our Own*
11. Working for Us—for a Change   109
12. Finding Out about the Community   120
13. Minding Their Business   131
14. Investigating the Investigators   143

Part 4: *An End to All That: Proposals for Reform*
15. A Revolution of Light   154
16. A Freedom of Information Act   163
17. Only the Beginning   176

Postscript   182
Index   184

ACKNOWLEDGMENTS

The material in part 4 referring to the United States was obtained from *Litigation under the Federal Open Government Laws* (American Civil Liberties Union Foundation, 1993) and *First Principles* (Center for National Security Studies, Washington, monthly). Permission to use both sources is gratefully acknowledged. I wish to thank also all the patient people on whom I have tried out my theories, and the electorate of the National University of Ireland.

1 INTRODUCTION

● ●

Not so long ago, in 1977, Wicklow Urban District Council was faced with an awesome dilemma. A woman was sitting in, listening to their discussions! This was, apparently, unprecedented, and the members weren't sure she was entitled to be there. Discussion continued for a few minutes, and it was eventually decided, somewhat uneasily, to let the 'intruder' stay. Unfortunately the *Wicklow People*, which reported the incident, didn't ask the woman what she thought of the whole affair.

Until recently many people in Ireland would have liked to pretend that that's a somewhat unrepresentative story. In fact it is an entertaining illustration of the instinct for secrecy that runs through all our private and public institutions. (I mean secrecy, not privacy. Anyone who has ever dealt with a state agency or with one of the banks will know that their secrecy and your privacy are not the same thing.)

While Wicklow's confrontation with *glasnost* may have occurred a few years ago, the instinct it displayed hasn't changed much. The events of 1994, encompassing the alleged sale of passports, the blanket of secrecy surrounding the tax amnesty, and the eventual fall of the Fianna Fáil-Labour coalition, illustrate this well. Never has public rhetoric been so laced with talk of transparency, accountability, and indeed information. How real all this is remains to be seen. What we can see now is that far more than a gesture is needed. A cultural revolution would be more appropriate. And this must cover not just central government but local government too. Indeed it will have to extend beyond all these into the various state, semi-state and quasi-autonomous bodies that affect our lives. Secrecy is everywhere. Cork, in particular, seems to have a severe secrecy affliction. Its county council has a reputation for obdurate secrecy in environmental matters; and a politically expedient task force set up some years ago to advise the Government on Cork's problems discovered that its final report was in fact a state secret, so the report was never published. It may (there's no certainty here either) turn up in the National Archives eventually. It's probably no more than consistent that my own employers, Cork RTC, have instituted new restrictions on access to governing body minutes.

It would be wrong to suggest that state bodies are uniquely afflicted by the secrecy obsession. It's a trait that characterises the entirety of what can best be described as the establishment. As well as the state, into that category the churches, the trade unions and of course industry and commerce fit comfortably. Building societies, for instance, in theory are mutual societies under the control of their members. They have nevertheless developed a web of secrecy, as a result of which the members can't even find out how much they are paying their directors. Commissions from insurance companies can be seen as not being important enough to be worth disclosing.

It is of course wrong that supposedly mutual societies like these can, quite legally, withhold so much from their members. But the building societies are doing no more than copying the rest of the corporate sector in believing that directors have a God-given right not to disclose to those who must pay them how much they are actually paid. Buy a Smurfit share and go along to its AGM and try to find out what each director is paid and you won't get very far. Large numbers of your fellow-shareholders will share your frustration. It won't be shared, however, by the small number of institutions, banks, insurance companies and the like that own the largest numbers of shares. They, after all, are equally intent on keeping their own shareholders, not to mention customers, in the dark. They are not, therefore, going to start asking for the sort of awkward information that might establish dangerous precedents for their own AGMs.

Your general sense of frustration won't be helped by the realisation that these institutions don't really own the shares they control anyway. They are in large part bought by your money and my money through the savings we make in banks, insurance policies, and pension funds.

So we end up with those who borrow money from us and those who claim to be accountable to us as shareholders in effect working hand in glove to make sure that we, whose money they make free with, will know as little as possible about what they're up to. And if it all goes according to plan, we'll get our relatively modest pensions or lump sums and they'll get very rich very quickly.

Commerce isn't alone in all this. We take our secrecy very seriously in Ireland, and all our institutions work to maintain it. The Catholic bishops, for instance, have developed a wonderfully leakproof structure in which all decisions taken by the bishops' conference appear to be unanimous. There is an extraordinary contrast between their secretive commitment to the appearance of unanimity and the open discussion encouraged by the Roman Catholic bishops in the United States. There, drafts of proposed pastorals are made public, and submissions are sought. These drafts are then debated in public by the bishops. In Ireland, we are told, 'extensive consultation' takes place. What this actually means is that the bishops meet in secret those whom they choose to consult. The contradictory result is that we end up with often eloquently worded calls for an open and participative society from an institution that is itself closed, exclusive, and secretive. This leaves their eloquence with a dangerously hollow echo, which the more perceptive bishops deny and the remainder ignore. But then they couldn't even see the irony in their decision to make a submission to Rome on the role of the laity in the church that almost all of the Irish laity never saw!

The church is not the only advocate of openness and participation that is remiss in its own practice. Trade unions too rush for cover at the first sign of trouble. Only when the leadership find it useful is serious debate allowed. Most awkward issues are 'referred back' to the executive to be debated in private. ICTU conferences carry this to the extreme, with members of the executive alternating between the platform, where they represent Congress, and the floor, where they make sure their own individual unions are kept under reasonable control. This doesn't prevent them passing ringing motions on censorship and freedom of speech, openness and participation, of course.

It makes a depressing picture really. The overwhelming impression I have of our national institutions, after twelve years of participating in them (and almost becoming one myself!) is of irrelevance, impotence, and secrecy, with the secrecy being the clear cause of the irrelevance and impotence. I don't mean that our institutions can't do anything. But they have failed in any systematic way to deliver a service or policy that will satisfy both the needs and the hopes of the people. They are not seen by most people as having much to contribute to the solution of our problems. In the area of politics and economics, unemployment and emigration emphasise that failure so much that it would appear that both have already been talked close to death. Most people would doubt that there is anything new to say on them.

In a way they are right. Most of the debate on these and other issues has been dominated by economic arguments. Even leaving aside my own conviction that most of what has been contributed to economic debate in Ireland has been ideologically loaded, it would be easy to believe that we have talked for too long, tried so many different policy prescriptions and failed so often that there is therefore no solution.

Unfortunately, even the analysis of failure is presented to us in economic terms, and indeed in particularly narrowly defined economic terms. The failure of our institutions to work is little talked about and never argued about. Little notice has been taken in the political arena or in the media of the possibility that institutional failure, not failure of economic policies, represents our fundamental problem, the media preferring to entertain us with endless stories about the frailties, supposed or real, of our politicians rather than of the institutions they are supposed to run.

The institutional failure has been noticed by a few, but even some of those who have noticed have only been prepared to offer limited proposals for change. They are usually proposals for changes at the top of the institutions, proposals for restructuring, for more 'hands-on' management, or indeed for a more 'market-oriented' management style. That would be the classic insiders' position. The insiders, after all, know far more about these institutions than we do. They decide in most cases what we are entitled to be told and can concoct a limitless list of excuses to justify secrecy. Indeed many insiders, bureaucrats and politicians alike, increasingly seem to believe that the removal or dilution of democratic accountability will increase the efficiency of our institutions. The rhetoric of fashion, of the market, is the current flag of convenience for these views. We are presented with images of inefficiency, lack of accountability, lack of commitment to service and to the 'customer'; this is the reason our institutions don't work. A good dose of the 'market' will change all this, we are told.

In this ideologically laced analysis, international evidence is ignored. The inconvenient evidence would include the fact that in health care, for instance, the American system—the most market-led in the world—is also the most expensive, while other state-run services, like those of most of Europe, are both cheaper and more efficient and, in terms of indicators like infant mortality, more effective. Many of these successful European institutions and services operate in societies where the right of a citizen to know is taken seriously. This can range from a simple right to know who is responsible and a right of access to that individual to the right to read and copy all institutional records that led to a particular decision. Surely the correlation between openness and quality is not just a coincidence.

In Ireland we are rarely trusted with the full information that is used in coming to a decision, or indeed any evaluation of the alternatives. We will see how this works in decision-making in the areas of health, welfare, environmental security, and indeed public administration, and we will see the parallels between public secrecy and secrecy in the private sector. And we will evaluate too the myriad implausible reasons given to us to justify this continuing secrecy.

THIS IS WHERE the real failure lies, in my opinion. Institutions that have failed because they refused to accede to the essential attribute of democratic accountability and public knowledge about their operations are being challenged by critics who, notwithstanding the evidence, choose to blame failure on the very democratic principles that the institutions have ignored or subverted. Images of bumbling and perhaps greedy politicians contribute effectively to this campaign, and unfortunately there seems to be an endless supply of politicians who wittingly or otherwise do a superb job of stereotype confirmation. Ultimately, though, they are not the issue, because in democracy politicians are no more than a means to an end. Democracy means control by the people, and that control can be exercised in many ways, among them the delegation of power to elected representatives. However we do it, though, it ought to be self-evident that control can only be exercised if the people know what's going on. I don't have to be an outstanding political scientist to demonstrate that Italy's problems arose not from democracy but from a lack of it, which left most ordinary Italians suspecting but unable to prove large-scale institutionalised corruption. Once the people had the proof, they were more than capable of dealing with the problem. So when 'reformers' advocate a dilution of democratic control in, say, the health services, they are in effect arguing for more secrecy and less accountability, and that will solve none of our problems.

I am convinced, from personal experience, from reading, and from listening to the experiences of other people, that those who hold power in our society withhold from us most of what we would be interested in knowing and indeed need to know. As we will see, governments withhold information from us and keep secrets about us. We have no way of knowing how much. They tell us, usually, that disclosure would not be in the public interest, though of course the public are never asked whether they agree or not! And they tell us also that they can't tell us very much about the *reasons* for non-disclosure, because that might give us some idea of what it was they didn't want to tell us! We will see that if they investigate industrial safety they probably won't tell us the outcome even if you or I complain.

They find out who poisoned our cucumbers but won't tell us, 'because of possible legal consequences.'

Private bodies also withhold information from us and keep information about us. Again we have no way of knowing how much. They justify their secrecy with claims of commercial confidentiality. Of course where public and private interact, in environmental matters or in the enactment of company or banking legislation or in the regulation of building societies, we get a bit of both!

We will see that there is a curious parallel between the attitude of the Government and that of the directors of companies and financial institutions. Both are very good on the rhetoric of personal freedom: the system calls itself a 'free' market, after all. Governments justify many of their less pleasant activities by invoking the need to defend our democratic institutions, that is, our freedom. Company directors and bankers will resist regulation and Government interference, again by reference to the 'free' market. We are, it appears, surrounded by people dedicated to defending and extending our freedom. Indeed freedom has developed an ever more extensive meaning. Even taxation is talked about as an intrusion on freedom. It's the same with hints at the reintroduction of exchange controls to inhibit speculation: personal 'freedom' would be affected, we are told.

The resistance of the corporate sector to proper disclosure is sweetly ironic. As the vanguard of the now triumphant 'free' market, they and their intellectual allies are very much the determiners of ideological orthodoxy. It is amusing, therefore, but also extremely threatening, to find that the defenders of the free market are in fact among the most active in subverting it. Market economics is based on competition and free choice. The first assumption then is that a potential purchaser of anything—goods, services, stocks, shares, mortgages—has full information. The reliability of a company, the integrity or greed of its directors, the environmental record of its overseas subsidiaries, the safety record of its products, are all obviously of considerable interest to market participants, that is, to the average citizen. All these are necessary if 'free' citizens, operating in 'free' markets, are to make their 'informed' choices. Of course. But while intellectually and practically necessary, such information could make life very difficult for those who run (and get rich from) such companies. Such discomfort is easily and conveniently confused with commercial disadvantage, which would clearly be bad for the company as a whole. So the information is withheld by the company as far as possible and by the Government where the company gets its way. This commitment to self-preservation and market power would come as no surprise to Adam Smith, who, while providing the intellectual basis for all future analysis of the market, was profoundly sceptical even two hundred years ago of those who participated in it.

Many of the great thinkers on politics were also sceptical of those who participated not just in the market but in the exercise of power generally. They had observed the almost universal abuse of power throughout history, and struggled to develop political institutions that would minimise, if not end, that abuse. The early days of the United States were marked by vigorous efforts to prevent the establishment of a standing army, because of the possibilities for abuse that it could provide. Those efforts failed, and it is at least a matter for debate whether the United States and the world would be better or worse places if a different decision had been made.

Our secretive institutions haven't evolved in a vacuum, of course. They are products of our society and its successes and failures. One of our successes has been our capacity to produce powerful charismatic leaders with broad national appeal. O'Connell, Parnell and de Valera are obvious examples. Each achieved a lot, but each, and particularly the last two, had a uniquely autocratic style of operation. It is clear from both Lyons's biography of Parnell and Bowman's account of de Valera and Northern Ireland that neither believed in trusting anything significant to paper nor in serious consultation even with immediate party colleagues. Lyons's account of the perpetual bewilderment of most members of the Irish Party with Parnell as they waited to be told what they were going to do next fits well with Bowman's frequent references to de Valera's determination to commit nothing to paper and to keep his counsel to himself.

Party policy was largely announced, not developed. Popular participation was neither envisaged nor indeed even considered.

That might have been no more than a natural consequence of circumstances and history. Dealings with the greatest economic and military power in the world at the time must have required considerable nerve and considerable skill. There may have been no room for the ideal degree of participation.

Unfortunately it appears as if that mentality, the perhaps necessary product of years of struggle, instead of being disposed of when the struggle ended was in fact institutionalised. We replicated legislation, as in the Official Secrets Act, that was produced elsewhere to defend military and security interests when in fact all we had to defend was the confidentiality of state examination papers. We didn't, unfortunately, think of producing legislation that dealt with our specific conditions, but copied others. We went on then to add our own gloss to that already censorious system we had inherited by introducing censorship laws. These were not too different from those of our nearest neighbour and of many other countries but were applied here with the zeal of fundamentalism that gripped us after independence. It is fashionable to attribute that fundamentalism to our religious traditions, but it seems to me that it was more a product of a sense of national purity presented as religion rather than a purely religious phenomenon. It's worth remembering too that the controversy about the infamous Mother and Child scheme, which had a large 'information' dimension to it, was as much a product of secular and medical conservatism as of church dogmatism. That controversy illustrated yet again, however, the unwillingness to trust ordinary people with information without the influence of an intermediary.

But of course these are the enlightened 1990s. All that is past history. Unfortunately, today is not that different. We still have censorship—and I can see no way round that if we wish to assert the right of women in particular not to be presented as playthings and indeed objects of hatred and misuse. Our censorship, though, often goes beyond that. It projects itself as being pro-woman but attempted after all to tell women that they were not entitled to the information necessary to make their minds up about abortion. Indeed until recently we had legislation in force that told us that information about some ways of preventing pregnancy was more acceptable than others.

We appear to be moving away from that era now, but as we do so we have extended our control in other areas. Indeed we can see a consistent logic to it throughout our history. The instinct is always the same: once a controversy starts we try to reduce the flow of information.

The operation of section 31 of the Broadcasting Act exemplifies this. It was first used to prevent RTE broadcasting interviews with members of or spokesmen for the IRA. It was later extended to members of Sinn Féin and indeed to a list of other organisations that were deemed to support the use of violence to achieve political ends. Sinn Féin, however, was unique among the organisations listed in that it had, and has, substantial support in Northern Ireland: it received 27 per cent of the votes in Belfast in the local election in 1993.

The gradual but enormous extension of the broadcasting ban is even now rarely discussed. At first it was confined to the operation of state-owned broadcasting organisations; some could see a logic in that. Later, though, it was decided to incorporate the equivalent of section 31 in the legislation that set up independent broadcasting. With that decision we introduced, without much protest, state political censorship of private media of communications. This meant that the only place where the views of the elected representatives of perhaps 35 per cent of the nationalist population of Northern Ireland could be found was in the newspapers.

For most of the establishment this was a quite acceptable position. Renunciation of the use of violence for achieving political ends was supposed to be a precondition for participation in democratic institutions; indeed the Supreme Court upheld and extended that view when it upheld the ban on Sinn Féin election broadcasts. This judgment in effect invited the state to extend section 31 to include all the media, including newspapers and magazines. The state did not do so, presumably because, while it knew that the print media would not object too vigorously to censorship of competing media, they would baulk at blanket censorship of themselves. They did, however, rationalise the existing censorship in terms of the alleged democratic precondition of an end to violence. This is a topic that needs long debate and perhaps a separate book but that must be addressed, even if somewhat cursorily, here.

Renunciation of violence has never been a universal principle of democratic acceptability. It is more often an excuse for exclusion, and is usually practised against those who are weak, both politically and militarily. After all, Ronald Reagan was accorded a warm welcome by many people to Ireland even as he financed an armed struggle against a government in Nicaragua that had won a free and fair election. The justification offered for this was usually that he had some kind of mandate; the connection between his victory in an American election and his use of force in another country was never clear to me. After all, Sinn Féin had won elections too. They had been elected to councils, and indeed to Westminster. They hadn't won a majority in an election, of course. So does that mean that minorities have no rights? Of course it doesn't. Everyone was, rightly, concerned that the rights of white South Africans should be protected after the ending of apartheid. We were in effect saying that a particular minority—supporters of Sinn Féin—had no right to use violence.

Everyone except Sinn Féin and its supporters appeared to agree on this. But why did 35 per cent of Northern nationalists see it differently? Why did they support, passively or actively, the use of violence? For most of the last twenty-five years— because of the operation of section 31—we didn't know. This information deficit and the inevitable demonisation of Sinn Féin that followed force me to draw what I believe are irrefutable conclusions.

The first of these is that the ban was a purely political decision, designed to make invisible a part—perhaps the most intractable part—of the Northern problem. That it succeeded is evident in the growing popularity of Gerry Adams as he is 'de-demonised' in the post-censorship climate. Arising from that is the inevitable feeling that section 31 may well have prolonged rather than reduced violence in Ireland.

My second conclusion is that section 31 as it was applied had less to do with the uniqueness of the situation in Northern Ireland than it had with the continuing desire of the state to keep a firm grip on the activities of the broadcasting media.

RTE, it appears, acknowledged something like this when it decided to appeal against a High Court decision that would have restricted the application of section 31. It must be unprecedented in a democracy for a branch of the media to appeal against a court decision that in effect reduced censorship.

In that atmosphere of secrecy, censorship and the threat of its renewal, we will attempt to explore the many ways in which we are kept in subjection. We will look at many of the areas that affect our lives most intimately, and see how little they really let us know. We will look at education policies that are made without laws and in secret, at health services where even the obvious reassurance of good communication is withheld from the sick. We will explore the various ways, in the name of democracy, in which democracy is diluted in the interests of 'national security'. And we will reflect on the ludicrous secrecy concerning environmental matters that we have imposed on us, in spite of an EC directive. We'll have a look too at equally ludicrous manifestations of secrecy in the state and the private sector.

Of course it is possible to find out more than you might at first imagine, so we'll look at ways of using the system to find out information even within the existing framework. But we will soon realise how much is withheld. Fundamental reform is what is needed, reform so sweeping as to necessitate institutional revolution. As we'll see, such revolutionary reform will not necessitate taking huge risks. We will simply be following the example of others by a commitment to transparency, accountability and decentralisation in the public sector. In the private sector we'll simply be trying to ensure that the market economy works as the theoreticians say it should.

Part 1
We Know They Know but Still They Won't Tell Us

2 | HOW THEY FORM US: EDUCATING IN IGNORANCE

• •

The policy of minimum accountability that we talked about in the previous chapter underlies the way education is administered in Ireland. Most of education is run without legislation and with limited public accountability. There is no legislation governing primary schools: they are run according to rules devised by the Department of Education that were never debated in public and are not even open to amendment by the Oireachtas. And yet the state spends many millions of pounds each year on primary education. Similarly, contracts are agreed with individual primary school teachers that are based on no legislation and may perhaps leave teachers in a much more vulnerable position than they imagine.

Through this non-legislative vacuum the state hands over untrammelled ownership of schools and land to primary school 'patrons'. Schools are legally owned by these patrons (usually the local bishop of either the Roman Catholic or Church of Ireland persuasion, depending on the denominational ethos of the school) and not, as many people think, by the Department of Education or the Office of Public Works. When a school is closed for one reason or another it does not revert to the state but becomes the property of the patron. In some cases the Department of Education may claim a veto over a proposal to dispose of a school, but it can't compel a patron to sell or hand over a school. We have a situation therefore in various parts of the country where schools are empty and other groups would like to use them but are refused. Most notable among these are the multidenominational schools that are seeking premises but are resolutely refused access to these empty schools at any price. Much of this power-wielding is, of course, done secretly, since neither the bishop nor the department are required to make anything public.

Even where a degree of public and parental participation is advanced, the ring of secrecy is preserved. Boards of management are supposed to run schools, and there is parental representation on these boards. But parents are a minority on the boards, outnumbered first of all by the bishop's nominees but also by the combined numbers of those nominees and the representatives of the teaching staff and the principal. This composition was agreed by the patrons, the department, and the teachers' union. It was then presented to parents, very often by the church that negotiated it, as the decision of the Government. Local parish priests profess ignorance of the rationale behind it. 'It's the department that makes the rules,' they say. Contradicting that assessment is somewhat difficult, since the record of these negotiations will remain secret for at least thirty years, or perhaps longer if a minister decides that it's not in the public interest to disclose it even then. It would be interesting to know what exactly the argument was that was used to justify the absence of any requirement that the patron's nominees even have children going to the school on whose board they serve.

The rationale behind the requirement that primary school boards must not discuss individual teachers' performance would be worth investigating too, but we won't be told about that either. Indeed it's difficult to discover even the simplest things about the operation of school boards. This is because it appears to be laid down that parental representatives may not be required by the parents who elected them to report back on the activities of the board! This is more than consistent with the spirit of a paragraph in the glossy (and ironically quite informative) document that the Catholic bishops make available to members of boards of management. It says on page 27: 'Members of the Board are required to keep confidential matters discussed at meetings …' and concludes: 'Where the Patron is satisfied, after due investigation, that any member of the Board infringed this injunction of confidentiality, he/she shall remove that person from membership.' This removal clearly applies even to the elected representatives of the parents.

Contradictions appear too in the process of appointment to primary school teaching positions. These are made officially by the board of management; but many national teachers I have spoken to are convinced that there is in effect a rigorous 'faith and morals' vetting by the local clergy. These are alleged to involve a parish priest reporting on the Mass attendance record and marital orthodoxy of applicants. I have known aspiring national teachers living in rural areas to go to the extreme of using addresses in towns just to frustrate the operation of this 'faith and morals' network. This may well demonstrate how ludicrous the network can be made to look, but it also illustrates the secrecy that can sustain it. Even if it were justified it ought to be stated and above board. Advertisements in the *Tablet*, the English Catholic journal, frequently specify that applicants for jobs be practising Catholics. It would be more honest and less sinister if we were prepared to do that here. The trouble is that our primary schools are meant to be open to children of all religions, and therefore any formalised procedure for the exclusive recruitment of conscientious practitioners of one religion might well provoke constitutional challenge.

But in the area of primary education it's not just at local level that we are excluded from the information loop. The Department of Education retains much of its old ritualistic suspicion of accountability. It is, of course, accountable to both the Comptroller and Auditor-General and the Dáil Committee on Public Accounts, which ensures that the department spends money legally, that is, according to the estimates approved by the Dáil. But the Comptroller and Auditor-General has no say in the decisions about criteria for expenditure under approved headings. As to educational strategy, however, we cannot hold the department accountable at all. We can have questions asked in the Dáil; but while these may well result in some extra factual information being provided, they will never allow us to assess the underlying strategy or the criteria that are applied.

Attitudes to Irish-language schools are an excellent example of this. They represent an extraordinary innovation both in educational philosophy and in attitudes to Irish, but there has been no public statement of detailed policy from the Department of Education. Of course there has been plenty of lip service to the concept, lip service that was often not too consistent with the department's own attitudes. The experience of the founders of one of the first of the 'new wave' of such schools illustrates this well. Scoil an tSeachtar Laoch was established in Ballymun twenty years ago by working-class people who wanted to deepen their children's sense of being Irish. They assumed that, given the official rhetoric, they would find things easy. As it turned out, it was only their resolute determination that got the school off the ground, a determination that had to match an unstated but obvious determination by the department not to allow the school to go ahead. This, of course, was never made explicit: it was always a matter that was being studied, or else there was a request for more information (often the same information over and over again). It was easy for the department to delay even then when there was a need for more and more primary school places. The public had no criteria by which to judge it, no rules that the department was to abide by, no standards that it was required to meet. We wondered at the time why the department appeared to be so hostile. Was it that they thought the language was dead? Was it that they thought the idea of working-class interest in the language was impossible or unlikely? Or was it hostility to the idea of detailed local involvement in education that they disliked? We won't know for years, or perhaps ever. We do know that Scoil an tSeachtar Laoch was a huge success. It eventually became so big that a second school had to be opened. The two schools between them will have about a thousand pupils.

The department appeared to do its best to delay the introduction of multidenominational schools. Again it never said what its objections were. It didn't even say it objected: it just found reason after reason to delay. And it has full freedom to do that, since criteria for decision-making or for establishing priorities either don't exist or are a well-kept secret. Correspondence from defenders of the status quo would make interesting reading and might explain the department's reluctance. But we'll never know, because it's all wrapped up in unaccountable secrecy. It is this secrecy also that facilitates one of the more peculiar aspects of educational financing, the prioritising of expenditure on bringing schools up to decent standards of sanitation and heating. It would not be difficult to establish and publish objective indices and to tackle the problem on the basis of greatest need. Instead it is left, in my view, deliberately vague, with proposals being studied endlessly and decisions postponed. This may be convenient for the politicians and ministers but is not much good for the image of our institutions. Once again we have allowed ourselves to be excluded from power. Proper standards would demonstrably be in the public interest and indeed the interests of those of our children who have to suffer these awful conditions and wait for a political favour to escape. Secrecy suits those who like to give the impression that they are dispensing largesse.

These issues are significant. Much more significant are the issues of educational standards. We know that the Department of Education has an inspectorate. We know that the inspectors visit schools and that our children are usually in some awe of them. But we will never know what the inspectors say about all or any of our schools. Do they comment on class sizes and their effect on our children? Do they comment on the ageing of our teachers, which must affect the quality of education? Do they identify schools that are underperforming, schools that place too much emphasis on the ubiquitous entrance exams? Do they assess the performance of boards of management? What do they say? We are not to know.

Primary education is supposed to be free. This is a visionary commitment in our Constitution and one that has served us well. It is hard to reconcile, however, with the 'local contribution' that every primary school must make as a condition of receiving capitation grants from the Department of Education. It would be fascinating to find out the reasoning by which the department convinced itself that these compulsory contributions were compatible with the Constitution. Have they legal advice to that effect, or are they simply chancing their arm? Similarly it would be useful to know how the department reconciles the constitutional right to withdraw children from religious instruction with its own insistence that religious instruction be all-pervasive in primary schools.

At second level the situation is in some ways worse but in some ways considerably better. There are at least the Vocational Education Acts, which outline structures of decision-making and of accountability, though parents and students get scant mention in them. But at least funds have to be publicly accounted for, there is some structure for the appointment of teachers, and the boards of management can deal with problems concerning teachers.

This at least is the case in the public sector. Matters are entirely different in the dominant private sector, and a large section of the public sector seems keen to co-operate in that difference. This is most emphasised in the uncertainty about the criteria of admission to second-level education. How many parents can say with certainty where their children will be going to second-level school? For the first child of many families there can be no certainty. This was emphasised in an extreme fashion by recent happenings in Limerick. There, an innovation that must at first have seemed progressive—the introduction of a common entrance assessment—turned into an exercise in unaccountable secret power. Parents in Limerick expressed a preference for a particular second-level school; they were then told where their children were going. The criteria by which this allocation was made were secret, unknown, it appears, even to the Department of Education. And this procedure included not just private secondary schools but also all the schools in Limerick that are officially part of the public sector.

While the Limerick situation is extreme, variations on it apply around the country. Some schools claim that they don't hold entrance exams. They run 'assessments to test pupils' abilities', they say. When you ask them why they have to do this, given the uniform curriculum that all primary schools operate, they give as many reasons as there are schools. And almost all insist that these tests are non-competitive! Nevertheless there are many examples of entrance exam or assessment papers that contain material that was not on the primary school curriculum. One wonders why. One also wonders why, if these exams or assessments were non-competitive, so many primary teachers felt obliged to drop everything except English, Irish and maths for the first six months of sixth class. One will wonder unrequitedly, because all these matters are confidential. Secondary schools are private schools; and most of the others aspire to be just as secretive.

And the mystery doesn't end there. Parents tell story after story about the denials that streaming exists in first year followed by the discovery that their children have all mysteriously ended up in classes of roughly the same examination performance.

There is much more we don't know about private, fee-paying schools. We know that the salaries of their teachers are paid by the state, so that the fees are essentially a topping-up to give the privileged a state-subsidised advantage. More mysterious is the manner in which the state assists in the building costs of these schools. It gives substantial grants, which vary between 30 and 80 per cent of the costs (depending on who you listen to). The criteria by which these grants are decided upon are difficult to come across. In Cork in the last ten years two such schools got substantial state funding at a time when schools in the non-fee-paying sector were having to survive in pre-fabs. These privileges are further extended by the mysterious application of covenanting to their fund-raising. This in essence means that the tax authorities allow contributors to make their donations from their gross income; in some cases this almost doubles the value of the contribution, at no extra cost to the contributor. The extra payment takes the form of a refund of tax paid by the donor, and the refund goes to the 'charity'. How it is possible to covenant money for the operation of a fee-paying school but not for a genuine charity—like, say, the Simon Community—remains a mystery. Even a question asked in the Dáil didn't clear this mystery up.

Secrecy is not monopolised by the fee-paying sector, however. Much of the determination of policy for second-level education is done behind closed doors. In many parts of the country agreements are reached about sharing school facilities, about which subjects may be taught in common, and about some sharing of teachers. Sometimes it is agreed to have only one school, sometimes to have shared facilities, and sometimes schools continue as independent entities. What criteria are used to determine how these decision are reached? We don't know. It is difficult, though, to believe that securing the religious ethos of the school is the central point of all this.

It is the same with appointment procedures to secondary schools. There are criteria for minimum qualifications, and the schools usually impose a 'faith and morals' condition for appointments to Catholic schools. But we don't know how this is adjudicated upon. Does it involve simply asking candidates if they are Roman Catholics, or is there more? Does the second-level equivalent of the primary school black-list exist, or is it more informal? We don't know. But there is even more we don't know. We don't know how candidates are ranked even if they survive the 'faith and morals' hoops. Is it merit, and if so how is it assessed? Is it influence? Do past pupils get special preference? Do the families of existing teachers get preference? The determined lack of transparency seems, to put it mildly, to contradict the very policy of participation and openness that the governing body for many of these schools, the Conference of Religious of Ireland (formerly the Conference of Major Religious Superiors), advocates.

Secrecy should be the last thing one would expect from third-level institutions. The universities, after all, are much given to expounding on their commitment to the advancement of thinking and the pursuit of ideas. And yet both they and their state regulatory agency, the Higher Education Authority, share many of the afflictions of the rest of the educational sector. Universities are overwhelmingly funded by the taxpayers. The difference between the proportion of running costs that the state third-level sector and the university sector get from the state is no more than a couple of percentage points; but the difference in accountability is enormous. And that's not to say that the state sector is a model of accountability.

University funding is allocated through the HEA. The authority has stated criteria by which it works out the staffing and funding levels that it believes are appropriate to university education. It also agrees on minimum building standards. One presumes that the Department of Education agrees with these criteria and standards. And yet the department is quite prepared to insist on lower standards of staffing, building and equipment for the non-university sector. The result is that a new Engineering School for UCD cost as much as a new RTC in Tallaght. There may be good reasons why this is so, but we are not allowed to make up our minds about this. It is, as usual, 'not in the public interest' to make it known. It's more likely, however, that there are no logical criteria in existence and that an ad hoc policy has been cobbled together. This is probably based on a slovenly acceptance of an academic snobbery that believes that universities are 'better' and somehow 'need' higher standards. How, otherwise, could we have a situation where the RTC system, supposedly dedicated to practical and vocational training, could have ratios of technical support staff to students that can be close to one-third of those for comparable departments of universities? How is it that universities can apparently afford to employ proper security, arts officers, ground staff and the like while the RTC system cannot? How is it that academic appointments by the RTCs need ministerial sanction, while those in the universities do not?

The universities will insist that to require them to seek such approval would inhibit academic freedom. But no such fear seems to trouble them when they accept large-scale corporate sponsorship for schools of business and the like. Where are the details of such sponsorship agreements? And then there is the whole area of academic research and academic-industry partnership research. Millions of pounds are expended in this area every year in Ireland. Much of it is well spent, and indeed my own opinion is that we could do with a lot more of it. Much good work has been done. Sometimes, however, this seems to be more by accident than design, because the process by which funds are allocated is difficult to fathom and to an external observer defies logic.

I am aware of circumstances where an application for funding was made to a state body and the applicant was informed that it was refused because of a lack of money. It subsequently became known that there were no more than three viable applicants, and a successful application consisted of a project identical to the one refused. Intriguingly, the successful one was nothing like as well prepared as the one rejected 'because of shortage of funds'. How in another case did the state end up funding two effectively identical projects within miles of each other? There may well be a logic to all this, but it would help all round if the criteria were made known.

Our practice contrasts with the scrupulous attempts at objectivity made by the EU. Applicants are assessed by independent assessors, who don't know the identity of the applicants. Based on these assessments, the applications are ranked and graded. Only applications that meet a minimum grading standard can be considered for approval. The grading is done independently of the final funding decision, and it is possible to refuse funds to proposals that are ranked equally with those funded. Nevertheless each applicant knows his or her ranking and can easily find out those of others. All this means that the public know vastly more about the selection criteria practised in Brussels than we do about those in Dublin. It is not, as applicants will tell you, difficult to get background information about research proposals from Brussels. It is possible to have informal discussions with relevant officials; indeed such discussions are encouraged. Similar clarity is not, unfortunately, practised at home. Indeed there are documented instances of information refused by state agencies being readily available from Brussels. I am led to wonder where precisely the 'democratic deficit' really exists. Is it in Ireland or in Europe?

There are often other problems associated with research. Students sometimes wonder who is funding research they are involved in. Sometimes they suspect that it may be for so-called 'defence' projects funded by the US authorities. Usually that information will not be forthcoming. Indeed when it comes to the US Defense Department, Irish institutions are far more subservient than their American counterparts. This emerged when the IIRS (subsequently Eolas and now part of Forbairt) made an agreement with the Pentagon to assess standards in

Irish enterprises supplying parts to American defence agencies. The IIRS refused to make the agreement public, on the grounds that it was 'confidential'. It was nevertheless obtained quite easily in the United States under the Freedom of Information Act!

Secrecy and non-accountability extend further, though, in the third-level sector, as an experience of my own illustrates. I served for six years on the Board of Management of Cork RTC. During that time a legal action was begun against the college, which ultimately resulted in the payment of over £150,000 in damages and costs to the plaintiffs. The final settlement was kept a closely guarded secret, and would have remained so had the Comptroller and Auditor-General not mentioned it in his annual report. Indeed it was long after I had left the board that I learnt that I was actually named in the statement of claim of the plaintiffs. During that period too an attempt to do a student project assessing the efficiency of the college's use of electricity was initially vetoed on the grounds that the college's electricity bills were confidential! The veto was overturned quite quickly, but only, I'm convinced, because the staff members on the board made a fuss.

Finally, of course, information on student assessments and the criteria by which projects and other course work are assessed are still difficult to come by. The Data Protection Act probably gives a student the right of access to information held on computer, but many authorities have prudently ensured that 'sensitive' information is kept in documentary form. This would also be true of the records of proceeding of college bodies and indeed of supervisory bodies. They have also to keep records that are on the right side of the law. In the light of all of this it can hardly be a surprise when it turns out that the Department of Education shows a reluctance to comply with the National Archives Act, behaviour heavily criticised in the most recent report of the National Archives Advisory Committee.

3 | FOR OUR OWN GOOD

● ●

Health, we are told nowadays, is not just the absence of illness: it is a positive sense of well-being. We are reminded often that people's recovery from illness is intimately related to psychological as well as physical conditions. People who are emotionally secure and reassured will recover more easily and more rapidly than those who are frightened or unhappy. A great deal of what is written about modern health and indeed about the modern life-style is devoted to extending this understanding of how we react to illness and to the stress associated with it. There is increasing recognition too that we can be affected by how other people feel about our illness.

Holistic approaches are the order of the moment, with most of our large hospitals at least nominally having policies that should ensure that a patient recovering from open-heart surgery and suffering the depression that often goes with that condition will have access to top-quality psychiatric care. There is, too, an increasing recognition of the role of pastoral care and counselling in helping people to cope with serious and, even more importantly, terminal illness. Both the AIDS crisis and the hospice movement have provoked a deeper understanding of the need to build up the human support side of health care. It may be a cliché by now, but health services are about caring as well as curing. The curing will proceed more successfully if the person being treated is comfortable and reassured and has a good understanding of what is being done and the reasons why.

Of course it is also true that, directly or indirectly, the citizen in receipt of health care is a paying customer. The paying may be by means of personal insurance, social insurance, or taxes, but it manifestly is not free. Patients are customers in receipt of a service, and even on commercial terms they are entitled to know what it is they are 'consuming'. They are entitled to know that what is being done to and for them is determined by a professional assessment of their needs and not by convenience, prejudice, or indeed a paternalistic belief that ordinary people are better off not knowing.

All of this was given formal recognition during Dr John O'Connell's period as Minister for Health when he unveiled what was described as a Charter of Patients' Rights. It is an admirable document. It says that delays are to be avoided and that patients have a right to care of the highest standard. It also says that patients are entitled to be told what their diagnosis is and what the proposed course of treatment is. Alternative treatment procedures are to be explained to patients, and they are to be given access to their medical records. In addition they are not to be used in any testing of new medication or other treatments or involved in teaching exercises without their consent.

The charter is prominently displayed in the outpatient and emergency departments of almost all public hospitals. It has, however, no legal force and guarantees nothing. No legislation came with the charter, nor was any promised. Medical records are not easily accessible, and it is no easier to get information than before, according to reports I have received. This may be yet another example of an apparent resolute refusal to treat patients as a priority, but it is more likely a consequence of the fact that overworked hospital staff are faced with too much work and too few resources. They concentrate on the practice of medicine and follow that by endeavouring to meet whatever statutory obligation they may have.

Aspirational documents, like ministerial rhetoric, are ignored or discounted by the overburdened work force in the health services. Most doctors, in fact, are not unhappy with the non-operation of the charter. Disclosure is not a profoundly popular policy with the medical profession generally. There is a widespread feeling that medical records could be misused if in the possession of poorly informed or indeed malicious people. Indeed there would be problems in enforcing a legal right to medical records for private patients, as the question of ownership of those records is far from clear. Many would argue that the records are the property of the doctor and that therefore disclosure cannot be enforced by the state, which is, as far as private practice is concerned, no more than a funding agency and contractor of services.

For perhaps 60 per cent of the population, then, medical records, charters notwithstanding, are in effect inaccessible, unless of course a court action is threatened or unless they are kept on a computer. As we'll see, Ireland was forced by international obligations to regulate computer-based records under the Data Protection Act, thus begrudgingly giving some access rights to information. Records kept on paper, however, are not covered by the act. So if your doctor uses a computer, even if it's only a word-processor where he or she stores letters and treatment records, you are entitled to those records. But most doctors, and other professionals, are well advised and will hardly store anything electronically that might put them at risk.

Medical records, of course, aren't just records of illness. They are also records of treatment and are indicators of choices made by doctors. They should show clearly how doctors arrive at decisions to use novel drugs or other treatments; but they would not say anything about how a doctor came to be aware of a new drug. Nor would they explain the criteria a hospital uses for assessing the appropriateness of new drugs. The Control of Clinical Trials Act requires hospitals and drug testing agencies to set up ethics committees to develop such criteria and to formulate a policy. Nevertheless in many cases even the membership of such committees is difficult to establish, and their records are, it would appear, totally inaccessible.

In the absence of documentary evidence we must rely on the titbits that are thrown to us. We know that the Department of Health has reminded doctors that they should avoid excessive reliance on the hospitality of drug companies. Such warnings are welcome, but they are no substitute for full disclosure. It seems to me that it would not be unreasonable for the public to expect to know the details of all research, travel and hospitality funding provided by drug companies for doctors and health workers. This may not be significant, it may even be negligible, but there is good reason to insist on disclosure.

The pharmaceutical industry spends more on the promotion of drugs than on research and development of new drugs. R&D is claimed to take up close to 25 per cent of the turnover of most drug companies, so the spending on promotion must be enormous. Since for most new drugs mass media advertising is not permitted, this promotion must rely on advertisements in professional journals and on direct contact with and marketing to potential prescribers. It could make for lavish hospitality. It could ensure generous sponsorship of medical functions and of research budgets where appropriate. All this could well be of enormous benefit in the care of patients, provided we are satisfied that objective criteria were used in determining the appropriateness of particular funding exercises. Perhaps such criteria exist, perhaps they don't. What is clear is that silence and secrecy only add to public suspicion. There can be no doubt that the public would be enormously reassured if they knew the full story and were satisfied that they were not in any way guinea pigs in multinational competition.

Secrecy seems to surround us here already and we haven't even touched the question of medical ethics generally, and in particular those controversial areas involving reproduction and sexuality. It is quite difficult for a woman to persuade most doctors in most state and voluntary hospitals to carry out a tubal ligation unless there is a clear medical reason, involving a threat to the woman's life from a further pregnancy. Even that grudging concession was only made recently and is by no means universally applicable. Who makes these decisions? The ethics committees, of course. How are ethics committees formed? We're not too sure. Have they rules, procedures, standing orders, minutes? We don't know. Have they equal representation by women? Perhaps, but since they are not required to make their membership known we can't be sure. Nevertheless it is this barely visible body, appointed by no formal statute, that orders medical ethics in most of our public hospitals.

Given the secrecy and the consequent lack of accountability, it comes as no surprise that most of these committees appear to come to conclusions about ethics that coincide with those of the one body in Ireland that really feels strongly about the prevention of sterilisation: the Catholic Church. When a Catholic hospital in Galway was sold to private interests, the Catholic Church, in the person of Bishop Éamonn Casey, insisted that the contract of sale include a commitment from the new owners that Catholic medical ethics would be enforced for ever in the hospital.

Though the priorities may seem strange, and the subsequent history of one of the protagonists may add to the sense of unreality, one cannot dispute the fact that they were legally entitled to insist on such conditions. The hospital was, after all, the property of an agency of the Catholic Church. The claim by that church of a right to impose similar bans in state hospitals is, however, very much open to question. It can't be challenged, however, because it is never owned up to or explicitly admitted. It is enforced in a more oblique fashion than that; and the ethical diktats don't just apply to sterilisation. For years most publicly owned maternity hospitals refused to dispense, or advise on, methods of contraception other than those that some people regard as 'natural'. The reason given—where one was given at all—was not one based on an ethical distinction nor on the ethical position of one church: it was that there was 'no demand' for the other kind of information, we were told. Indeed after Barry Desmond introduced his amendments to the contraception legislation (or the family planning laws, as they were called) he inserted a clause allowing health boards to sell non-medical contraceptives in hospitals. Health board after health board decided not to do so, the reason usually cited being 'lack of demand'. How this paucity of demand was discovered we weren't told. And how it squared with the dramatically rising demand for contraceptives in the country generally was never explained either. Nevertheless the ban was maintained.

So it goes on. You know that there are other influences, other agendas, but they are unrecorded and often unstated, though the result is clear. You end up feeling that, in the words of Shane MacGowan, you are attempting to argue with 'a bottle of smoke'.

All this obfuscation doesn't just apply to sterilisation and contraception. It applies with a vengeance to anything to do with the termination of a pregnancy. This is supposed to be illegal in Ireland. The real position is a classic example of how law, morality and secrecy become so enmeshed that most people end up totally confused.

Perhaps the first thing that needs to be said in an endeavour to clarify these issues is that notwithstanding the fudging that goes on, pregnancies are terminated in Irish hospitals. They are terminated by the removal of a woman's womb on occasions, and they are terminated too in recent times by microsurgical removal of an ectopic pregnancy. The foetus in an ectopic pregnancy cannot survive, and the condition will ultimately result in serious haemorrhaging, which can be fatal. It was dealt with previously by surgical removal of the ruptured tube; now it can be dealt with before the woman's life is threatened by removal of the fertilised ovum. It is difficult for anyone with a practical view of life to see how this can be other than the deliberate destruction of a foetus. We are assured that this is not the case. Perhaps it isn't, but we are not to know the decision-making structure that is used, nor the guidelines offered to doctors in a situation like this. Do all maternity hospitals operate similar procedures when dealing with ectopic pregnancies? If not, how do individual hospitals deal with that situation? How do they deal too with the critical choices about when to intervene if malignancy appears in the womb of a pregnant woman? If a woman is twenty-four weeks pregnant, do they wait till the foetus is at least potentially viable, or do they intervene immediately? We hear the vague generalities epitomised by the 1983 amendment's 'equal rights' clause, but not the arguments nor the rationale behind refusals to intervene.

We do not hear much either about the procedures that are made available to rape victims by some hospitals, albeit on a slightly hazy basis. I'm referring to the dilation and curettage (D&C) procedure, a classic Irish solution, echoing the use of the contraceptive pill in times past as a 'cycle regulator'. D&C, as the term implies, involves dilation of the womb and scraping the inner surface. It is routinely done after a miscarriage to avoid the risk of infection and future complications. In Ireland, rape victims are sometimes 'diagnosed' as having a complaint that necessitates a D&C, and conveniently all the contents of the womb are removed. At the time the procedure is performed no-one can be sure whether the woman is pregnant: the procedure ensures that the problem never arises. It may well be necessary in some cases on purely medical grounds, but it is nevertheless carried out in semi-secrecy or in a flurry of nods and winks, because of the uncertain ethical position. There is a feeling that if ethics committees were asked to rule on such issues most would severely restrict the practice. I am aware, as are many others, that it is done, but the cloak of secrecy emphasises the uncertainty that surrounds this whole area. It also underlines our lack of knowledge of how services ostensibly provided for our health are regulated and indeed withheld without our knowledge.

If one can see a historical reason for the fudge on these sensitive issues, the reason for an even more complete blanket over other health-related areas is clearly the preservation of the power and influence of the health establishment. There is, for instance, a widespread conviction that health board obstetricians almost always attend deliveries by their private patients but often leave straightforward deliveries by public patients to the undoubtedly highly skilled nursing staff. There will be records in every maternity hospital in the country that could sort this out. Why not publish them?

In a similar vein it would be perfectly possible for health boards to ask medical card holders about the quality of service they receive from GMS doctors. They could ask them whether the GMS doctors respond quickly to house calls, or at all. Medical cards are renewed regularly, and questions like these could be added to the renewal form. A similar procedure could operate in hospitals, particularly now that they have procedures for collecting money from most of their patients, and no extra paperwork would be involved.

There are in addition more fundamental information deficits

and indeed information suppression. We know that there have been substantial cut-backs in health services in recent years. Hospitals have been closed and thousands of jobs lost or not filled. It is often close to impossible to get a hospital bed for a public patient in other than extreme emergencies. It is similarly impossible to find long-term care and accommodation for public patients who are chronically ill. There are, of course, some beds available for both categories. They are allocated presumably according to some criteria or other; it would be useful and helpful to families to know what the criteria are. It would also be of great help to GPs, who are often stuck between inadequate hospitals and frustrated relatives and patients. Nevertheless these criteria, if they exist, are not made public. The result is that most people believe that political influence is the key, and politicians are not inclined to disabuse them of the notion. The perception of power is almost as important as the actual possession of it. Doctors and health authorities could clarify the matter, but they choose not to. Like so may others in our society, they will advance many reasons for the secrecy, from privacy to professional ethics, but it is easy to conclude that they know, consciously or otherwise, that the monopoly of information is the source of their power and is also a wondrous diluter of criticism.

Another consequence of the reduced public provision for the elderly has been the dramatic increase in the number of nursing homes. They are clearly profitable, and no doubt many are of an excellent standard. Nevertheless there have been well-documented horror stories. These are now meant to be avoided by the powers of inspection and licensing given to health boards, which can close nursing homes if their standards are inadequate.

All nursing homes must be inspected from time to time. The inspection is done by health board officials, who presumably compile detailed reports on the standard of care. They will obviously find different standards even among those that are deemed 'adequate'. It resembles a detailed and expert equivalent of the inspections that Bord Fáilte do for hotels and guesthouses, out of which comes a 'star' system.

For elderly people and their families the information compiled by the health boards would be invaluable in choosing a nursing home. The trouble is that they won't publish it. So off we go again. Every health board in the country is busily spending taxpayers' money inspecting and reporting on nursing homes but resolutely refusing to share the information they compile with us! Health boards, it appears, are sensitive bodies and wouldn't like to offend the owners of approved nursing homes by letting potential consumers know about their failings.

That's probably not so surprising, because health boards are notoriously sensitive when it comes to criticism of their own services. The Eastern Health Board has been reported to have instructed its social workers not to accept referrals of homeless children from Father Peter McVerry, who has been a particularly vigorous critic of theirs. At least two other health boards have made strenuous efforts to stifle criticism of their services. According to the *Irish Medical Times*, the Western Health Board has circulated a draft code of what they called 'ethics' which in effect forbids medical staff to supply anyone, even their own trade union, with information about the board's services without prior approval. The North-Western Health Board followed recently with a similar effort. The *Irish Medical Times* (7 January 1994) carried a report claiming that the board was endeavouring to silence the president of the Irish Hospital Consultants' Association using a directive similar to the earlier attempt of the Western Health Board. They told all their consultants that they were to refrain from all public comment on the board's services. They won't succeed there either, I'm sure, but they will ensure that the hundreds of doctors in insecure junior and temporary positions will keep their comments to themselves.

That, of course, is what the health boards like. They rush for cover at every possible opportunity. When the great aspirational *Planning for the Future* document was being prepared, all the health boards made submissions beforehand—secret submissions, of course! These submissions represented the boards' considered position on the future of the psychiatric services. It would obviously not be in the public interest to let the public know what a public body proposed to do about the public's health care.

More recently the Southern Health Board developed a plan.

They decided that they wanted all funds for public voluntary hospitals in their region to come through the board, voluntary hospitals being at present directly funded by the Department of Health. The decision to seek this change was taken at a private meeting of the board, without any prior public discussion. The reasons the change was being sought were kept private too, and the hospitals in question read about the proposal in the newspapers.

All this makes one nervous about the new powers the health boards are getting under the Child Care Act. Among other things, they will be responsible for assessing residential child care facilities in their areas. The Department of Health will have a similar function with regard to such facilities run by the health boards. Reports of such assessments would obviously be of great interest to the public; but given the current position on reports on nursing homes, there is no guarantee that they will be published.

But then we shouldn't be surprised at the attitude of the health boards. Their role model is presumably the Department of Health, and it has never been the most communicative of departments. When I was in the Seanad it was the only department where all queries from Oireachtas members had to be dealt with through the minister's office. The Health Education Bureau was abolished, being replaced by the anodyne Health Promotion Unit. There was no great saving in money, but the department was firmly in control again. Suspicions were aroused when Dr James Walsh was moved from his position of AIDS co-ordinator.

The catalogue of secrecy, of attempted suppression of criticism on a scale that not even the Department of Justice would contemplate and the obvious lack of enthusiasm for disclosure flies in the face of the Patients' Charter. It increasingly flies in the face of modern understanding of patient care, but it is consistent with attitudes generally within the state service. In the health care area that whole attitude is epitomised by the experience of Keith Best and his mother. Mrs Best fought a twenty-year court battle to win compensation for her brain-damaged son, who was finally awarded over a million pounds in compensation. No sooner was that bureaucratic battle fought than another began, when Mrs Best ran into problems with the court authorities about the new home she proposed to build, following the best professional advice, for her son. They appeared to think it was too dear. The system appeared to be suggesting that a woman who could have bankrupted herself seeking compensation for her son was now going to go off and waste the compensation she fought for for twenty years. Why? We don't know!

4 THE AIR THAT WE BREATHE

● ●

Clichés abound when protection of the environment is discussed. No-one is against it, either in the public or the private sector; everyone now claims to be one or another shade of green.

Clichés are more or less essential in the political world. That is probably a natural hazard of politics. Nevertheless in environmental matters even the normal excesses are overloaded. The speeches are now so standardised as to be predictable.

The pattern is to begin with a proclamation that our Irish environment is our greatest natural asset, our most precious resource, and of course is not for sale. (I heard a suspiciously similar set of clichés directed towards young people in the late 1970s and early 1980s. And then of course we exported them.) This is usually followed by a reiteration of our determination to allow only development that is in harmony with our environment. Then usually comes a reference to the EU Declaration on the Environment. Until recently, as if to balance reassurance, this used to be topped off with a ritual warning that of course we can't allow a Luddite or extreme environmentalism to inhibit developments that would generate 'much-needed jobs'. A colourful phrase about comfortable middle-class environmentalists often went down well.

It took a while for the system to realise that many people didn't believe these commitments were genuine. This has generated an addition to the ritual, which takes the form of a declaration of the need for 'transparency' in environmental decision-making. Environmental decision-making is going to set the highest standards; there will be a degree of public participation that will win it confidence and a level of independent enforcement that will win public approval. What more could we want?

We would be entitled to believe then that the process of decision-making in the environmental area would be a model of openness. And indeed the Department of the Environment likes to give that impression. It runs a high-powered environmental information service, ENFO, that supplies attractive information leaflets and a reasonable collation of published statistics on the environment. It is actually, within its brief, extremely good, and it is staffed by enthusiasts who will try very hard to help you to make the best use of any information the agency has at its disposal.

Understandably enough, ENFO deals with the national or international environment; it cannot be expected to provide a comprehensive local service. Local services, though, are the touchstone of environmental 'transparency', because for most citizens the environment is exclusively or at least primarily a local matter. It's the developments in our locality after all that determine our environment. And local planning offices are open to the public, with the intention, one would presume, of complementing the work of ENFO.

Unfortunately it doesn't work like that. Planning offices have a fixed and delineated brief and can only be required to make quite specific information available. Some may do more than this, but by and large it's only worth your while visiting your local planning office if you want information on current or former planning applications. Environmental data has to be sought elsewhere.

But even the most aware among us would hardly regard a visit to the planning office as an important daily routine. We will make the effort when we think it's important, when we need to know about something that's likely to happen in our own localities. But we must first be made aware that something is planned. 'Transparency' surely begins with that. We need and deserve to know what's planned.

Unfortunately, most local authorities have given up publishing lists of planning applications in the local papers, as a cost-saving measure. (The applicant, of course, usually has to put an advertisement in a newspaper, either local or national, but the national paper can be the *Cork Examiner* in Donegal or the *Irish Press* in Cork, making it extremely unlikely that any but the most vigilant will spot it.) You'll probably find them in your local public library. But the ending of newspaper advertising, however it's explained, suggests at the very least a declining commitment to engage the public in environmental debate. It also amounts to further evidence for what I believe is an almost unwritten law of public administration: that the scale of the rhetoric is inversely proportional to the scale of the resources. So it is that as the talk of 'transparency' spreads and develops, the resources for 'transparency' dwindle.

But suppose you still find out about a plan, and go to inspect it. The first thing you will notice is that, because of a shortage of funds, hours of opening are probably significantly less than they were a few years ago. It will probably be impossible to call in on your way to or from work: planning offices open late and close early. So even where openness is actually legislated for, an escape from work will have to be organised if you want to claim your rights.

Nevertheless you struggle on and confirm that there are plans for industrial or other development in your area. It turns out to be a complex proposal, perhaps a small business manufacturing printed circuit boards, or a local entrepreneur expanding a food-processing plant. You're no expert, but your local residents' association will have no trouble finding one. So you ask for a copy of the maps and plans associated with the application. 'Can't be done,' you are told: the applicant holds the copyright on the plans, and you can only get a copy from him or with his permission!

At this stage you're missing work, trying to sort out who it is that will give you a copy of the plans, and reminding yourself that you have to get your objections in quickly. So it's quite possible that you will be late. Even if you're not, the planning authority may go ahead and give permission. You can get a copy of the decision, but you could still be without a copy of the nub of the application if the applicant decides to be unhelpful. The permission, of course, is a response to the application and refers to the application at length: but it doesn't contain a copy of the application. So you aren't really going to be in a position to call in any expert adviser who hasn't got the time to go and stand (usually) at the desk of a planning authority and read the plans. And of course there is the minor detail of a charge for a copy of the decision. For a six-page document I was charged seven pounds, which must make Cork City Council one of the most expensive photocopy providers in the world.

At this stage a working definition of transparency in the planning area is beginning to emerge. You are not prevented from knowing about and inspecting planning applications. You can have a ludicrously expensive copy of the decision, but you must depend on the good will of the applicant for a copy of the most basic document. While you organise yourself to get around that inconvenience you discover that recent legislation has reduced the time allowed for appeals.

Let us assume that you are still in combative mood and want to proceed further. You can appeal to An Bord Pleanála. This again must proceed quickly. You can *ask* for an oral hearing on the appeal, at which the applicant can be cross-examined by you or your representative; but you are most assuredly not guaranteed one! So you might like to know what criteria An Bord Pleanála uses to decide whether an oral hearing will be granted or not. They won't tell you; and indeed an employee of the board who told you could be committing a criminal offence.

At an oral hearing an inspector from An Bord Pleanála hears all the evidence and the cross-examination of witnesses. He or she then reports to the board. They make a decision, refusing or granting permission, or granting permission with conditions. There is no appeal against their decision except on a point of law. Quite extraordinarily, though, An Bord Pleanála do not have to publish the detailed reasoning behind their decisions. They can overrule local planning decisions, in the process dramatically changing a local environment, and yet never have to explain themselves. They can choose to make people very rich by overruling local planners, and never explain themselves. And they can refuse permission and never have to explain themselves.

Nor do they have to abide by the recommendation of their own inspectors. In the case of Radio Tara ('Atlantic 252') the inspector's report became available to the public, and it turned out that he had done what the overwhelming majority of the people of County Meath wanted: he had recommended that permission be refused. The members of An Bord Pleanála overruled their own inspector, for reasons that they had no obligation to make public.

Somewhere in our progression, transparency got lost. We are confronted by secret decision-making, based on secret reports that can be accepted or rejected for reasons that almost always remain secret.

The contrast with normal judicial procedure is worth looking at. In the High Court or the Supreme Court the case is argued in the usual way. The High Court judge gives his or her decision and the reasons for it. This decision may be appealed to the Supreme Court. The Supreme Court will again hear the arguments; it will in time give its decision. With one rarely used exception (that of a bill referred to the Supreme Court by the President) the individual decisions of the five Supreme Court judges will be given separately. As a result we will know whether the decision is a majority decision or unanimous. We will know the reasons why each individual judge adopts a particular position. And all that published material will become the stuff of further arguments in later cases. Precedents will be established that, while not binding, will usually be treated with great respect in later judgments. In this way a body of case law is developed, which assists in interpreting the written law or the Constitution.

Of course it would be both unreasonable and impractical for An Bord Pleanála to have to adopt all the formalities of the courts for many of the issues that reach it. The board deals with many issues that are fairly trivial, after all. What is not unreasonable and seems eminently sensible to most people is that it ought to make public the conclusions of its own inspectorate, together with the arguments on which its own members make their decisions. A body of 'case law' would help future developers to meet the criteria set by the board.

As we will see shortly, the judicial analogy I have just drawn is not something I thought up, and in fact has given us a considerable insight into state attitudes to freedom of information.

Secrecy extends further, though. If someone appeals to An Bord Pleanála and an oral hearing doesn't take place, then a very one-sided view of 'publication' operates. The original applicant will be supplied with a copy of any appeals lodged and invited to reply, as will the local authority. If you appeal against a decision, you won't know what arguments the applicant uses, nor get a chance to oppose them, nor will you see the response of the planning authority, nor the views of other applicants. Indeed it is one of the glorious inconsistencies of the planning process that for an oral hearing everything must be made public, while the refusal of such a hearing results in secrecy. Why should a local authority's views on a planning appeal be secret? Since logic doesn't indicate a reason, then surely culture does. This is the culture of secrecy, whereby that which is not required by law to be published will remain secret.

This extends into other areas of planning. Planning authorities used to be responsible for issuing all water and air pollution licences. For a designated range of industries these are being replaced by integrated pollution control licences issued by the Environmental Protection Agency. This agency is based in County Wexford. One can inspect the application in the agency's offices and usually at local authority offices in the region where the licence applicant operates. Copies of the application will be made available at a price of £250 per copy. In an area like Cork Harbour this could cost a local pressure group thousands of pounds. Some companies will supply copies of their application to interest groups, but they are under no obligation to do so.

Nevertheless you can appeal the licence (difficult though this might be without a copy of the application). Your appeal is to the EPA again. It is not clear yet how much information you will get in response to your appeal (fee £100). What is clear is that you will have to hurry, as you will only have three weeks in which to appeal. When the three weeks include the Christmas holidays you could end up with less than a week in which to prepare your appeal. For other non-designated industries, air and water pollution licences will continue to be issued by local authorities.

As always, applicants for a licence can appeal to An Bord Pleanála. So can any third party (for a fee, naturally!). You may feel that your local authority was unduly lenient, or poorly advised, or that it failed to consider the smell that you have lived with for the past ten years. You would like to know the arguments that your local authority is using with An Bord Pleanála. You won't be told.

Neither will the local authority members be told, in contrast to national decisions and national issues, where the bureaucracy has no right to withhold any information from the Government. The Government may decide not to seek information, or may decide to restrict information to certain of its members; nevertheless those decisions always lie with the Government. They generally decide to be secretive, and obsessively so, but they have the power to change it if they wish. Albert Reynolds recently made his engagement diary public. Local authority members, it appears, have no such power.

Some years ago strange blue flames began to be seen on Cork City Council's dump on the Kinsale Road. An environmental problem had occurred and needed urgent attention. It happened because buried organic waste had begun to decay out of contact with air. In contact with air such decay produces carbon dioxide, water, and possible traces of sulphur dioxide. None of these is explosive, though each has some negative environmental consequences. Without air present, however, the same organic matter decays to produce methane and hydrogen sulphide. Hydrogen sulphide is quite toxic and has an unmistakable 'rotten eggs' smell. Methane has no odour but is highly explosive; it is the major component of natural gas. Smell and explosion risk together meant that action was needed. Consultants were called in. They produced a report.

Council officials at first refused to give council members copies of the report. Various reasons were given: confidential information, capable of being misunderstood, open to misrepresentation, etc. The members resisted, however, but eventually it took a 'section 4' motion by Michael Martin TD to force the council to make the report available to the members.

Planning, of course, is not just about plans: it's also about the enforcement of plans. If certain conditions are laid down then they must be enforced, or else the whole process is meaningless. These conditions may be straightforward in the case of something like a housing development: the developer must provide roads, sewers, and so on; a specified housing density must be met; trees must be preserved or planted. Most of these conditions will be visible, and local opinion will help ensure that they are enforced.

In the case of industrial development it's not so easy. Conditions relating to the visible environment can be enforced locally. Local residents will also ensure that conditions about noise, traffic and so on will be more or less observed. But it's not noise or traffic that most concerns local opinion. People worry most about what's being emitted into the air and water. They are assured that the highest standards are applied in planning approvals, but they can't determine whether such conditions are met: complex analytical and control equipment is required to do that. So planning approvals insist on the monitoring of effluent, with regular reports of effluent quality being provided to the planning authority. They specify appropriate analytical methods and control procedures. They also usually specify a strategy that must be adopted if the treatment procedures fail. This varies, but should extend as far as shutting down the plant if serious pollution is likely.

Information on all this is supplied regularly to the planning authorities. They will be told what effluent concentrations are. They must be told if limits are exceeded. They must be told of any incidents that could result in environmental damage. All this is as relevant to the lives of local people as noise, or dust, or visual amenity. The only difference is in the way it is obtained. And yet until late 1993 most local authorities did not make public the monitoring data supplied by industries in their area. Arguments about commercial secrecy were usually brought forward; but the result was always the same. No details were published. The public were reassured that conditions were being met but were not given the details. It's only when a smell problem arose that the public were allowed to get involved. Unfortunately not all toxic substances, and few carcinogens, smell like hydrogen sulphide!

This is the position that people have found themselves in since environmental awareness dawned about fifteen or twenty years ago. The struggle for trustworthy information and a suspicion of collusion between industry and local authorities created an increasingly hostile public opinion. The revelation during the Hanrahan case that South Tipperary County Council had taken no legal proceedings in connection with numerous breaches of planning conditions by Merck, Sharp and Dohme further deepened that hostility.

The official response has been to at least pretend to change all that. The establishment of the Environmental Protection Agency and the EU Directive on Freedom of Information on the Environment are meant to reassure us. They will undoubtedly change some things for the better; the margins of secrecy will be pushed back a little, but not far. There is no information revolution round the corner, because even where they aspire to openness, both are victims of the Irish secrecy culture too. (The painstakingly slow and unhelpful attitude of Cork County Council has been well described by Greenpeace, Cork Environmental Alliance, and Earthwatch.) And there is much that neither aspires to cover at all.

If the EPA were to model itself on the American EPA, then much would be revealed to us. That body leads debate, has no compunction about enforcing tough environmental regulations (as the Smurfit Corporation discovered to its cost), and operates under the Freedom of Information Act. Our EPA will unfortunately be quite different. The legislation that sets it up contains a section on secrecy that makes the unauthorised disclosure of any 'confidential' information in the possession of the agency a criminal offence. And to avoid uncertainty and ambiguity, 'confidentiality' is defined: information will be 'confidential' if the agency says it is! The only qualification is an indirect reference to the EU Directive on Freedom of Information on the Environment. Matters that the Government believes to be covered by that directive will not be 'confidential'!

That minor qualification was not in the bill when it was first published. It was inserted into the bill in response to vigorous criticism from inside and outside the Oireachtas, including a number of amendments from myself. It is a useful insight into official attitudes that a Government amended legislation to ensure that the EPA could not keep secret anything that it was legally obliged, in the Government's eyes, to make public. At the same time the Government refused to indicate the kinds of information the EPA was allowed to treat as confidential. It did not refer to any information that the EPA would possess that might be outside the scope of the directive. Information on newer technologies, or information on workers' health, or reports of EPA inspectors, can be kept confidential for as long as the EPA wishes.

Confidentiality is a reasonable concern for the management of any agency. It cannot allow a situation to develop where every employee can divulge whatever he or she feels like, whenever he or she feels like it. Nevertheless it is only in the state sector that the leaking of information is treated as a criminal matter. If an employee of a chemical company leaks commercially sensitive information, he or she can be disciplined, fired, or even sued; but the Gardaí will not be involved unless there is an element of fraud involved. However, if the same information came into the possession of the EPA (in a licence application, for instance) and was leaked, the employee of the EPA would be subject to far more severe penalties than the employee of the company.

And there is no exception provided for an EPA employee who leaks information that the agency might have suppressed but is of public importance. If the EPA says it's confidential then for the employee the choice is silence or prosecution. Indeed it's doubtful if even the disclosure of information covered by the EU directive would be a defence. Matters of interpretation are left exclusively to the EPA directors. We could probably rely on an Irish jury to do the right thing, but it would be no substitute for the right to know.

I will be accused of going on about the way things used to be. The Directive on Freedom of Information on the Environment will 'change all that'. And it might have. The directive itself is expressed in general terms, full of the people-oriented rhetoric that characterises such documents. It expresses a right to freedom of information on the environment, and lists the usual reasons that entitle a Government to refuse information. These restrictions apply to commercially sensitive information, to breaches of privacy, to incomplete work, and to national security matters. They also apply to the internal documents of Government and judicial bodies. It's a list that, when looked at in general terms, seems perfectly reasonable. But of course EU directives, while having the force of law in all EU countries, are put into practice through national legislation, or some variant thereof. Irish Government departments have tended to implement EU directives by circular on occasion, and sometimes by secret circular! On this occasion they couldn't. This was because the EPA Bill ultimately contained a clause that obliged the Government to implement the directive. It was yet again an interesting reflection of official attitudes that for a long time the Government resolutely refused to change the legislation so as to make implementation of the directive on freedom of information obligatory, even though it was obliged to do so.

Probably the most extensive bolt-hole manufactured by our leaders is in connection with An Bord Pleanála. The Department of the Environment has tried to classify it as a body carrying out a 'judicial function'. Thus all information held by the board would be exempt. In other words, if the Department of the Environment has its way, An Bord Pleanála can carry on its merry way, ignoring its own inspectors if it wishes, overruling local authority decisions, and not having to give us any explanations for its decisions.

Mind you, they are not prepared to insert all this into the regulations. Instead this is dealt with in the guidelines that accompany them. A friend of mine in Earthwatch told me that when they discussed this with officials in Brussels, 'they fell around laughing.' Indeed it is perfectly possible that a challenge to this interpretation would result in a court decision to throw out the daft interpretation attempted by the Government. But court challenges cost money. The state has plenty, environmentalists little. So in the meantime what we have is a decision by the Government to give the status of a judicial body to an institution that is not obliged to operate by the judicial norms of openness and cross-examination.

We still won't know what local authorities say when confronted by appeals on air pollution licences. Nobody will know what An Bord Pleanála's technical experts say. What's more, if you appeal against a planning decision, the applicant will (quite properly) be allowed to comment on your objection, but you will not be allowed to respond to those comments. In a court it would be a bit like being allowed to question a person once and then being told you had to leave the court and take no further part. The other parties can say what they like about your case, but you are silenced. This is exactly what happened to Earthwatch recently. They appealed against a decision by Dublin City Council in connection with a development by the ESB at the Poolbeg station. An Bord Pleanála refused an oral hearing (no reasons, absolute discretion). Earthwatch made their submission, and the ESB were invited to comment on it. Earthwatch then asked to see the ESB's comments. They were refused! Naturally they were also refused a copy of the report of the Bord Pleanála inspector who considered their appeal. All this happened quite recently, in the era of 'freedom of information'.

What are described without any sense of irony as the 'freedom of information' guidelines don't just attempt to exempt An Bord Pleanála. It's doubtful if you'll get your hands on any correspondence that may have taken place during the consideration of a planning application. And of course if an applicant supplies extra information, for instance about its overseas processes, or about its financial position, you probably won't get that either, because it looks as if we're going to be told that the planning process itself is a quasi-judicial body!

There are other defects and omissions too. The procedure for appealing against a refusal of information is far from clear, while the attitude of local authorities is disappointingly so. (Dublin County Council refused to release information about emissions from the Yamanouchi plant in north County Dublin on the grounds that it was commercially sensitive. It turned out that the information was permanently available to any casual visitor at the factory entrance.) And our faith in the new-found culture of openness isn't helped when we find that some of the bodies covered by the directive are not accountable to the Ombudsman. They are therefore fairly free to be as obstructive as they wish until someone takes them to court.

They didn't have to do it like that. The EU directive was an obligation that had to be met. The exemptions contained in it were permitted, not obligatory. The Government didn't have to accept all of them, and didn't have to put the broadest possible interpretation on them. For instance, we give public authorities up to two months to provide information (the maximum permitted under the directive), while in Denmark (and in the United States for freedom of information requests generally) it's ten days. We could have allowed access to public sector data-bases, but we didn't. This will slow down the process and increase the cost. Given the miserably restrictive attitudes already shown, this amounts to another device to delay and increase the costs involved for the applicant. And the citizen still won't be allowed a copy of the maps and plans that go with a planning application, because the regulations don't apply to information that is already 'required to be made available, whether for inspection or otherwise, to persons generally.' So, since you can look at it, you couldn't possibly want a copy of it.

That's what transparency means, then. It means that one obstacle is taken away and others are invented instead. Is it a coincidence that the delay allowed to local authorities in providing information is a month longer than the time limit for appealing to An Bord Pleanála? Is it really intractable problems with copyright that prevent us getting a copy of a planning application's maps and plans? Is it some principle of fairness that we don't know about that withholds so much of An Bord Pleanála's information from us? What is there in the state's environmental data-bases that means the public can't get access to them? What extra burden would be imposed on An Bord Pleanála if they had to publish the full written reasons for each of their decisions? And why has such a plethora of extra charges been introduced recently, including the charge to be paid for seeking an oral hearing? Why, apparently, has An Bord Pleanála never awarded costs?

We know there is no reason to justify all this secrecy that is of any benefit to us. There is a benefit for the system, though. If we don't know then we can't contradict them.

5

KEEPING US SAFE

● ●

'Security' is an enormously potent word in politics. It's a word that political leaders always feel comfortable making speeches about. Such speeches are usually well reported too, because the media seem to find security in one form or another eternally newsworthy.

Ambivalence in definition helps to add to the universal interest. For instance, 'green' economics makes a distinction between 'needs' and 'wants'. The former are part of ourselves, the latter are induced by circumstances, advertising, or society. This is very much at variance with conventional wisdom, particularly that of the post-communist 'victory of the free market', where our wants and our needs are taken to be synonymous. Nevertheless this alternative view of ourselves still identifies 'security' as a fundamental human need.

Even though the definitions may vary, it says something for the power of the concept that political figures ranging from Ronald Reagan to the Green movement are happy talking about it. We are all, whether conscious or otherwise, it appears, in a state of semi-permanent insecurity. So it is that even though these varying (even contradictory) definitions contribute to both the coincidence and the conflict, we all have strong and often passionate views on the issue. It is no surprise then that the political system, whether green or red or blue, has always been aware of the importance of references to 'security' in winning consent for various ideas, proposals, and sacrifices. Security can also easily be made to mean the same as law and order, and tough talk about law and order has never cost a politician votes.

There has hardly been a generation that wasn't carried along on a wave of law and order or security emotion. It's an area where there is always an issue, and usually a scapegoat. The Germans were the target in the early part of the century, quickly followed by the Bolsheviks and then after the war by the 'communist threat', which reached its climax in McCarthyism and enjoyed a mild revival under Reagan and Thatcher. Now of course it's immigration and Islamic fundamentalism and the ubiquitous 'terrorism' that threaten that hard-to-find entity known as western civilisation.

Global 'threats' apart, each society has its individual fears and prejudices. Those who control us know them well. 'Communism' and 'pagan England' worked well for years but are hardly much use for the future. Nevertheless they were effective in their time and were used to justify the most ludicrous activities by the security services. Recently declassified Government papers show that in the 1940s the Gardaí kept a close watch and reported back to the Government on the activities of the newly formed Irish Housewives' Association! Other equally innocuous groups no doubt kept many a garda late for his dinner.

One can only conclude that the state is overwhelmingly nosy, inquisitive, and insecure. It is probably true of all states, but manifestly true here in Ireland. That, of course, in a democracy is hard to admit. You can't say that, as a matter of course, the state opens your post, listens to your phone calls, monitors the meetings you attend, and wants to know what's going on inside every organisation that has not got the protective cloak of the establishment wrapped round it. Nor can you introduce powers of arrest, search and detention without a pretext. But given our collective sense of insecurity, which the state does its best to foster, a period of discomfort or indeed a real threat will inevitably arise.

Then the state either draws up sweeping 'emergency'

legislation (almost invariably described as temporary but that survives from generation unto generation) or sets up a branch of the security services that is accountable to nobody. In the past we had the famous case of Barney Casey, who, it was believed, was shot while attempting to escape from the Curragh internment camp and whose inquest was never completed. Today our courts are more active and vigilant, and we have ratified the European Convention on Human Rights; so a somewhat more subtle approach is required.

Subtlety, of course, is relative. It is true that we have no more Barney Caseys, but we have much that should concern us. The most extensive of the state's secret powers lie in the Offences Against the State Act and its amendments. This act allows internment without trial, but that's a much too blunt instrument to use in less than extreme circumstances. And we have not got, comparatively speaking, anything like a serious security emergency in this country. (Washington has more murders annually than have occurred in the whole of Ireland in perhaps the past ten years. The Mafia, by comparison with the IRA, is a real threat to the Italian state.) We have a problem, then, but not a security emergency. Nevertheless the Offences Against the State Act has been invoked to end trial by jury for large numbers of suspects.

That, of course, doesn't affect the average citizen. We have had only one proven spectacular miscarriage of justice in the last twenty years. What should worry the ordinary citizen is the attitude that the proclaimed emergency can engender among some members of the Gardaí. In some cases it is difficult to understand their motives.

When a young student left a meeting I had chaired, he was stopped by two men in civilian clothes who identified themselves as gardaí. They demanded to know his name and address. He asked what would happen if he refused. 'We'll arrest you,' they said. 'On what grounds?' he asked. 'On suspicion of membership of an illegal organisation,' they said. Having supplied them with the requested information, he returned to the meeting and told me what had happened. He was obviously frightened. I went out and complained to them. They hopped into their car and drove away.

Since much of the work of gardaí that is related to the operation of the Offences Against the State Act is regarded as secret, we don't know a lot of what goes on. But some statistics are available. One significant one shows the change in the application of the act over the years. Twenty years ago perhaps 90 per cent of those arrested under the Offences Against the State Act were subsequently charged with an offence. Nowadays, even though perhaps ten times as many people are arrested annually, not much more than 10 per cent are charged with an offence. (In recent years the Department of Justice has refused to supply a figure for the number of those arrested who are later charged, so our supply of information is even more restricted.) We have had a dramatic increase in arrests under the act and an equally dramatic drop in the proportion charged. There is some evidence that a similar turnaround has taken place in the use of search warrants under the act.

During a debate on law and order in the Seanad I asked the then Minister for Justice, Michael Noonan, if he could explain the change. He said that terrorists were getting tougher and had developed sophisticated anti-interrogation techniques. Given that a person can be charged with membership of an illegal organisation simply on the opinion of a chief superintendent of the Gardaí, it's hard to understand how all these allegedly hardened terrorists were not at least charged with IRA membership.

A more likely explanation is that these arrests are being used for information-gathering purposes. One person I know was detained some time after he and I had been drinking together. Ostensibly his arrest was part of a national hunt for a well-known subversive. He was asked where he had been earlier that evening, and told the gardaí that he'd been with me. He was released without charge and without anyone checking with me, but not before he'd been thoroughly quizzed on my political opinions. Others who have been detained found that most questions concerned their involvement in campaigns like that against the Criminal Justice Bill or in various referendum campaigns. Some people I knew in CND complained to a senior Garda officer about surveillance; the officer, who I know to be a very decent man, assured them that he realised that they were not up to anything illegal 'but the Government likes to know what people like you are doing.'

These are anecdotes, but there are lots more that could add to the impression that some gardaí interpret the law quite flexibly. This, they believe, allows them to put a liberal interpretation on the Offences Against the State Act. Under the act a garda must have a reasonable suspicion that a person has committed an offence under the act before they can be arrested. Similarly, in order to obtain a search warrant for arms, a senior Garda officer must have a 'reasonable suspicion' that arms are present on the premises to be searched; theoretically your home can't be searched 'just to have a look.' Nevertheless the behaviour described above is hard to reconcile with any reasonable person's understanding of that requirement.

The feeling that some of the Gardaí have given themselves considerable leeway is added to by other experiences of acquaintances of mine. One of them, a young woman, interrupted the Fine Gael ardfheis during Garret FitzGerald's leadership address, and was removed. She continued to protest outside and was told by gardaí that she'd be arrested if she didn't go away. She didn't go away and was arrested, on what she was told was suspicion of membership of an illegal organisation! She was never brought to court and was subsequently paid damages by the state in settlement of a claim for unlawful arrest.

A couple I know who were active in the hunger-strike campaign had their home searched: the warrant said for arms. The gardaí found no arms but took away large numbers of letters the couple had exchanged before they lived together. They also took a large quantity of condoms that the couple were storing for a pro-contraception campaign.

This 'flexibility' is not confined to interpretation of the Offences Against the State Act. During President Reagan's visit to Ireland a group of women set up what they called a peace camp in sight of, but a safe distance from, the US ambassador's residence in the Phoenix Park. They were promptly arrested and taken to the Bridewell, being offered various explanations for why they were arrested. The Bridewell is not very pleasant at the best of times. By that Sunday night, with thirty frightened and worried women crowded into a small number of cells, it was positively revolting. Along with Michael D. Higgins, I visited the women there. They complained that they had not been allowed to make any phone calls. The women were never convicted of any offence, and almost all were subsequently paid damages by the state in settlement of claims for wrongful arrest.

Power is dangerous if it's not accountable. The Gardaí have powers to arrest, question, search and detain us if they have reasonable suspicion. The Minister for Justice has power to allow the interception of telephone conversations and letters if the Gardaí request him or her to do so. Again reasonable suspicion is the test. Unfortunately it is obvious that at least some gardaí have evolved a very liberal test of what constitutes reasonable suspicion.

And because we can't prove them wrong, they can continue to get away with it. We can't prove them wrong because they rarely have to tell us, or indeed anybody outside the security establishment, what the basis for the suspicion was. Almost invariably if a garda is asked why a person was arrested or searched, they will claim privilege. They will claim that in the interests of 'national security' they are unwilling to tell a court or a jury how or why they formed that suspicion. Judges rarely refuse claims of privilege, so you won't find out there. The alternative if you're sufficiently aggrieved is to make a complaint to the Garda Complaints Board. Their procedures are slow and tedious. You may ultimately have the satisfaction of winning, but you won't learn much more.

Alternatively you could sue for unlawful arrest. There appears to be a good chance, but no certainty, that they'll settle out of court, and you'll be a little richer but no wiser. But they'll take their time. They may contest the case and claim privilege again. Fortunately a jury may not believe them as easily as would a judge, and you could well win the case. Whatever you do you won't find out their reasons, or whether they had any reasons at all. You might deter them a little.

But at least when it comes to search and arrest you will know that you were dealt with unfairly. When it comes to phone tapping and opening letters you can't even find out if they did it.

Ministers will offer smooth assurances that these things are kept under strict supervision and that no-one's phone will be tapped except for the most pressing of reasons. But they will never tell you if your phone is or even was tapped, which suggests that recent legislation to regulate tapping isn't going to make much difference. If they won't tell you what's happening it's difficult to see how you can complain, not to mention sue.

And of course ministerial denials need to be treated with a degree of healthy scepticism. I learnt that many years go when, after a housing demonstration in Dublin, the then Minister for Justice assured the Dáil that no batons were drawn by the gardaí. My delicate and bruised testicle proved otherwise, but I wasn't in much of a position to do more than learn the value of scepticism. I'm inclined to suspect, therefore, that those gardaí who, in the interests of 'national security', interpret 'reasonable suspicion' so flexibly must also have a fairly flexible attitude to the application of electronics to a simple job like listening in to phone calls. Modern technology makes it much easier. Gone are the days when a physical connection to a wire was needed to allow you to overhear another person's calls.

All this is regularly denied, of course, but since it's not the practice to make records available, ever, it ultimately depends on what you think the state's attitude to secrecy and privacy really is.

It would be wrong, of course, to think that only the Gardaí have the power and the inclination to pry, listen in, and put you under surveillance. Army intelligence has considerable powers too. These powers are similar to those of the Gardaí in the area of phone tapping and the like but are less commented on. This is presumably because the army hasn't got powers of search and arrest and is therefore less likely to penetrate our consciousness.

But the army has other secrets too. It is extremely coy about weapons purchases, and refuses to discuss in any forum, including the Dáil, the number, type or effectiveness of many of its purchases. This silence is maintained even when accurate information can be got from other sources. Some years ago I discovered through *Jane's Defence Weekly* and *World Missile Review* that the army had purchased a number of surface-to-air missiles.

According to the journals, similar missiles had been purchased by some of the Nordic countries and others in the Middle East. Despite this the Department of Defence was still less than forthcoming. My later discovery that the missiles purchased were unreliable in wet or misty conditions may have had something to do with their coyness! Even so, Ministers for Defence have continued to refuse to discuss the matter.

Other agents of the state also have considerable powers. Customs officers can detain you, search you, and ask a doctor to strip-search you if they suspect you are carrying drugs. Officers of the Revenue Commissioners can dig out a lot of information about you too.

All these powers given to all these agencies may well be necessary. The problem is that the exercise of many of these powers is not accountable in any simple way, other than perhaps by an enormously expensive court action. (The delay in bringing Nicky Kelly's case to the Supreme Court arose because he had first of all to raise the money.) The real solution would be to insert an element of independence into the assessment of suspicion, even after the event. It might amount to no more than allowing a judge, in private, to assess the information available to the Gardaí, army, Customs, Revenue, etc. Judicial guidelines could be produced to assist the various agencies, and people could be told routinely that their phones had been tapped and that an independent assessor had approved of the action.

Arguments against a degree of independence or of judicial scrutiny are usually related to 'national security'. It's always argued that the greater the number of people to whom information is made available the greater the risk of information being leaked. It's a plausible argument, until you consider its implications. Garda evidence is presumably recorded somewhere. So someone put it on paper. Most of this evidence is available to the Minister for Justice and to the Government's Security Committee. It's presumably passed from garda to garda, and is available to the Department of Justice too. It must be the same for information available to the army, Customs and Excise, and other agencies. It passes through lots of hands, not all of them senior or necessarily secure. So the argument that there would be a security risk involved in allowing a senior judge or an ombudsman-type person to review the information is more than a little shaky. And it collapses completely when we remember the antics of some of our Ministers for Justice.

So why the obsessive refusal of accountability? Obviously, and almost by definition, we don't know, but there is evidence from other countries to suggest a possible motivation. In Britain, for instance, recent legislation makes it an offence for anyone to make public an illegal act carried out by the security forces where those acts would otherwise remain secret. In the United States in the 1980s the Reagan administration made strenuous efforts to amend the Freedom of Information Act so as to prevent the disclosure of illegal activities carried out by law enforcement agencies. And the US Supreme Court has ruled that government agencies are free to do things outside the United States that would be illegal within it. The French government found it easy to make heroes of and indeed to promote the murderous bombers of the *Rainbow Warrior*. In the process they cynically broke an agreement they had reached with the government of New Zealand—an agreement reached after threats from the EU against New Zealand agricultural exports.

Our Government not only tolerated but in effect supported the French government in its illegal activity abroad. So why should we believe that things are all that different at home? If governments are unwilling to take reasonable steps to let us see that the powers of their security forces and other agencies are operated within the law, then we must conclude that they either have something to hide or are reserving to themselves the possibility of doing things in the future that they would like to hide. It leaves plenty of room for 'flexible' interpretation of powers if no-one is really accountable to anyone. Since the arguments from a national security perspective are so fatuous, that's the only conclusion we can draw. We'd be doing no more than our fellow-democracies either do or would like to do.

Remember too that those who keep us safe can see threats to national security everywhere. Even the newspaper you buy every day could cost you six months in jail—in the interests of 'national security', of course. That's because the Offences

Against the State Act defines a seditious document as one that describes any illegal organisation as an army. So if your paper contains any mention of the IRA you could be in trouble: that section of the act is not defunct either.

Mind you, what we have seen here only describes the somewhat precarious situation of a citizen under the law and the Constitution. Those who don't qualify under that heading— immigrants and asylum-seekers in particular—are infinitely more vulnerable. Refugees from China's murderous dictatorship have been detained in Mountjoy for up to a year without trial or court appearance on the basis of (as you'd expect) secret information. Aspiring asylum-seekers at one of our airports are alleged to have been assaulted on occasions, and many hopeful visitors have been refused admission on criteria that appear to have heavy racial overtones.

On two successive occasions I had to make a ridiculous fuss with the Minister for Justice to ensure that young Asian students from Shipley College in Bradford were given entry visas. They wanted to travel to Ireland from Britain on brief educational tours. These were young teenagers who were legal residents of Britain but were, under our immigration policy, apparently suspected of wanting to abandon family and education in Britain and remain on in Ireland. Mind you, the immigration officials didn't say that. They didn't say anything! Nevertheless a brief fuss via the Minister for Justice's office changed the decision on each occasion. Indeed on the second occasion these young people, previously suspected illegal immigrants, were admitted to Ireland without passports. This was because their passports were still here in Dublin for the purpose of having the visas organised on the day they left Bradford. So they ended up being admitted both visaless and passportless!

It is, of course, impossible to find out why these refusals took place. I suspect that the first refusal was a random application of a state policy that believes that all Asians are suspect and must be deterred. Are names tossed into a metaphorical hat and a few picked out? Are the few refused just to see what might happen and to deter all others? We probably won't ever know. The best we could hope for is that all hints of racial discrimination would be denied. It's a pity really, if only because I'd like to find out the reason for the second refusal. It looked awfully like a punishment for the fuss that was made the previous year, a reminder that complaining gets you into trouble.

So that's our security service. It merrily pretends to protect our democratic freedoms but contains within itself, apparently, many who are happy to ignore at least the spirit of some of the law that underpins those freedoms, and we have an immigration policy full of echoes of the old-style police state when it comes to dealing with 'blacks' and other non-people.

6 KEEPING THE POOR IN THEIR PLACE

That poverty is powerlessness would be the consensus among those who study, talk about and work with the poor. I'm not sure that the poor would agree entirely: most poor people that I know would still see shortage of money as the real definer of poverty. What would be universally agreed is that poverty causes powerlessness, and poor people are in effect powerless. And it's obviously because they are powerless that the welfare system treats them the way it does.

Welfare services, like all public services, are not isolated from society generally. Both the people who work in them and the politicians who ultimately are responsible for them are parts of society. Indeed, in theory at least, they are servants of society. They are fed their ideas by the usual sources, and most develop the same sort of perspective on the recipients of public services as the rest of society.

That common perspective usually means that the way you are treated by public services generally, and the welfare services in particular, is ultimately a matter of how you are perceived by society. Pensioners, for instance, are usually treated well, and interviewed in private by officials who have both the time and the inclination to explain their rights to them. Others—single mothers for instance—can find that attitudes change. Years ago I remember an old priest thundering against the introduction of the 'unmarried mothers' allowance'. We were now, he said, 'subsidising immorality.' I'm sure that widely held view showed up in the attitudes of the welfare agencies. In those days too single mothers were 'encouraged' to give their babies up for adoption. Tolerance grew with the years, though, and we renamed the scheme the lone parent allowance, reflecting both reality and a new, more benign attitude to unconventional family situations. Now we appear to be changing again. Moral judgments are back in fashion, and the rules will probably change along with the attitudes of those who administer them. Single parents are already getting a hard time in the United States and Britain; we in Ireland are surely in for another lurch in the direction of the new consensus. The operation and administration of any scheme echoes what politicians and administrators think are public perceptions. These perceptions sometimes change the rules, but more often they affect the way the rules are applied or enforced, particularly when it comes to disqualifying recipients from future benefits.

One consistent disqualifier is 'cohabitation', a concept that appears simple to define. Even so in Ireland it was only defined in quasi-legal terms quite recently by a working group set up by the then Minister for Social Welfare, Michael Woods. It has, nevertheless, been a disqualifier since long before the lone parent allowance was introduced. It has applied to recipients of widows' pensions since such pensions were introduced! However, while cohabitation is easy to understand and even define (though Michael Woods's discomfort with the explicitly sexual concept of cohabitation was obvious when the matter was discussed in the Seanad), it is somewhat more difficult to prove. It is reported, but unconfirmed, that an overnight guest of the opposite sex once a week is all right but that two or more nights is not. But, of course, we don't know.

It used to be that you were told nothing about how the conclusion that you were cohabiting was reached. Fortunately some progress has been made. Officials are now warned about the principles of natural justice and must supply some details of the evidence used in their adjudication. Of course their guidelines for this operation are rarely or at best only partly available.

At least in the case of cohabitation it is individuals who are the victims of secret evidence-gathering. Many recipients may avoid any penalty, either because they obey the rules or because they aren't caught, or because, as is often the case, officials find the whole business too distasteful and don't bother. It's a pity then that no-one found an exercise in secret evidence-gathering and private trial aimed at an entire community too distasteful. And that again presumably reflects society's attitudes to the community in question. Travellers are the victims of every imaginable discrimination, from the refusal to allow them housing to the refusal to allow them even to buy groceries. If you overhear Garda radio conversations you'll often hear them referred to as 'knackers', and even the most ostentatiously 'liberal' political groups cannot be relied upon to remain silent when the going gets rough. Nevertheless overt prejudice and structural discrimination against travellers ought not to be found in the public sector. We have had commissions, reports, plans and reviews, all of which called for action and all of which were welcomed by various Governments. The public sector, at least in policy objectives, pretends to be fair; and for a while it used to be fair. That was until scapegoats were needed to pacify the anti-welfare lobby.

The travellers were probably the first victims of that lobby. It was alleged, but never proved, that some travellers were signing on in more than one place, and sometimes north and south of the border as well, and thus claiming double benefits. The Department of Social Welfare investigated. They decided that there was a problem and came up with a solution. Every person 'of no fixed abode' would have to sign on in their local labour exchange or Garda station at 11 a.m. on Thursday. They used the phrase 'no fixed abode' to give the impression that the action was not directed against travellers; but the department has always refused to pay any welfare benefits to people who have not got an address. So a person who is of 'no fixed abode' cannot get welfare at any time, even at 11 a.m. on Thursday. Homeless people, for instance, know this well and will always give a hostel address, even if they're sleeping rough. Indeed they do this often with the knowledge, if not the encouragement, of officials of the department. In spite of that, homeless people were never affected by the Thursday morning directive. It was used against travellers only.

The effect has been to brand travellers as a separate subspecies, under collective suspicion for welfare fraud, and in the process go a long way towards confirming all the prejudices of the settled community against them. I and others have raised this prejudiced decision inside and outside the Oireachtas. We have been offered various bland rationalisations; but not a shred of evidence has ever been made available to me or to any travellers' representative to support the claims made. The department simply says that they are satisfied that fraudulent claims were being made by 'persons of no fixed abode'. Michael Woods even suggested that the travellers enjoyed the social side of meeting every Thursday morning! When I said he reminded me of a white South African saying that blacks 'preferred to live with their own kind,' he got very annoyed. But then perhaps he was annoyed by his own effective admission that, propaganda notwithstanding, it was travellers only who were required to sign on at 11 a.m. on Thursdays.

And so an entire community with a distinct cultural identity has been branded as criminal. (Needless to mention, the Gardaí have never been able to find evidence to prosecute people for this criminal offence.) They have no right of appeal against that stigmatisation and no way to deny the 'evidence'. They are told that a secret report, adjudicated on in secret, was the basis for the decision. The report contained 'irrefutable evidence', we were told. But no-one was allowed to see it. It's all so implausible that it led me to wonder whether there was a report at all. Perhaps it was another of the 'everybody knows' stories so widely told by the rich about the poor. Perhaps it was a convenient way of taking the heat off the Department of Social Welfare and finding conveniently unpopular scapegoats. And of course it made it easy for other, perhaps equally prejudiced state agencies to keep an eye on the travellers. You can always find them at 11 a.m. on Thursday morning. This procedure has since been revised but is still a fine illustration of how our system operates.

Whatever Michael Woods's rationalisations about anti-traveller prejudice might be, neither he nor his temporary successor, Charlie McCreevy, even pretended to rationalise the collective punishments that are imposed by the Department of

Social Welfare on the unemployed. They denied that they exist at all.

Being unemployed is wretched. It shouldn't be necessary to say that, but unfortunately it is, because of the hostility that unemployed people find directed against them by so many of the so-called experts of the economics profession. The process under which you are assessed for unemployment assistance or benefit makes it that much worse.

To qualify for unemployment assistance you have to undergo a means test. That test first of all requires you to make known all your assets, savings, and so on. Also, your parents' means will be assessed if you're living at home, no matter what age you are. And if you live away from home you'll have to prove that you *can't* live at home before they'll leave your parents out of it. There is a very simple reason for this. If you live at home you are presumed to get 'benefit in kind' from your parents, and that's treated as means, and your payments are reduced. Thus the commitment of the Department of Social Welfare to the maintenance, well into middle age, of the sanctity of the family!

If you apply for unemployment benefit you don't have to go through that process. However, whether you apply for unemployment benefit or assistance you have to satisfy the department that you are 'available for work' and 'genuinely seeking work'. These requirements are part of the 1993 Social Welfare Act. What they mean is, unfortunately, not explained anywhere: it is up to the department to interpret them. It would help to remember that these two requirements originated in the great days of low unemployment (now redefined as 'full employment') of the sixties and early seventies. In those days there was a shortage of teachers, plumbers, builders, labourers, and so on. It was reasonable to say that no-one had to be unemployed for very long. So the legislation was drafted to ensure that unemployed people went and looked for the jobs that undoubtedly then existed.

But that was in the days when 50,000 people out of work was regarded as scandalous and when 100,000 was regarded by Jack Lynch as a level that should result in the Government losing an election. It's different now. So it would be nice to know that rules drafted for a period of nearly full employment are applied differently now. As usual, we don't know! And as usual again we can't find out. Anecdotes abound that the department, of course, says are not typical, but notwithstanding their confidence they won't tell us any more.

Some studies have been done on the 'availability for work' requirement. The Coolock Community Law Centre says that this requirement weighs particularly heavily on women with children. The department's officials are always ready to ask women about who will mind the children, a question rarely if ever directed against men. During the great Jobsearch exercise some years ago women were told ('asked', the department says) to report for training for a payment not much greater than the dole. Since you couldn't employ a childminder with what you get on the dole and feed yourself and your children, many of these women refused. They were deemed 'unavailable for work', even though even the most poorly paid job would leave a woman in a position to pay someone to mind the children. Of course the department denied that it was policy to disqualify people who refused to accept Jobsearch offers. But they still wouldn't publish the guidelines under which it operated.

In other areas the penalties were less discriminatory but just as severe. Some people who found the perpetual idleness hard to take went back to school, and were told they were no longer available for work and disqualified. People who decided to help out with a local community association or voluntary organisation were also adjudged to be 'unavailable for work'. Essentially you were told to be at home all the time in case someone called to check up on you—except that you weren't told that or anything else. You were just supposed to know, presumably.

You also had to *prove* that you were genuinely seeking work. This might seem fair enough if it meant that you had to go to interviews for jobs and reply to ads for jobs, and the department and its allies were helping you to do this. But it doesn't mean that at all. It means that you are told you're not doing enough. You must try harder. How hard? They won't tell you. You must travel further. How far? They won't tell you. So if you're a building worker you'll have to go around various sites, almost all of which have a large *No vacancies* sign on display, and look for the foreman and get some proof from him that you asked. You'll have to persecute other local employers, and produce proof that you did it. And it has to be identifiable employers: letters to box numbers don't count. The department denies all this, but they still won't tell us how it's really organised.

A study I did of the application of these requirements showed that they were not applied evenly throughout the country. Severity of application also varied from time to time, even at the same place. Many unemployed people I've spoken to believe that whenever there is a fuss about welfare abuse, the pressure rises and they're told they're not doing enough. Many think that it is also a cyclical affair, with each location putting on a bit of pressure every so often.

So are these regular assaults planned? Are they part of an overall strategy, or are they simply a reflection of bursts of zeal by labour exchange officials? We don't know.

I pursued this issue throughout my period in the Seanad. It was never much reported, presumably because the journalists weren't affected by it. Of course advertisers aren't much interested in the unemployed either. We did, though, get detailed ministerial responses, in which we were assured that officers were trained to be sensitive in dealing with these matters. Michael Woods assured us that particular efforts were made to ensure that there was no discrimination practised between men and women. In fact he told us at the end of one debate that he had had new guidelines drawn up to guarantee this and other matters. He assured us that he would make sure that things were done fairly. He was positively eloquent in his passion for justice. So Tony Gregory asked him in the Dáil if he would publish these fair and just guidelines that he had dealt with so eloquently in the Seanad. 'It is not the practice to publish them,' Michael Woods told him.

Secret power doesn't end there for the unemployed. They are allowed to appeal, but again they are not provided with the evidence. They are told under which category they are disqualified, but not the evidence on which it is based. People who were involved in campaigns for the rights of the unemployed were disqualified on the grounds that they weren't available for work. In a number of cases disqualification followed their participation in demonstrations outside labour exchanges, but no-one was going to be so blunt as to connect the demonstration with the disqualification. So they appealed, the ritual of secret evidence was gone through, and they were reinstated. But it made you careful about future demonstrations! And, of course, since you never knew the evidence you couldn't prove anything.

The suspicion that there are no real guidelines is added to by the way the appeals procedure works. An appellant can seek an oral hearing of an appeal, but this is not guaranteed. At an oral hearing the appeals officer should be accompanied by two advisers who can advise on, but not participate in, the decision. The claimant is also entitled to bring an adviser. This could be a trade union official, a person from the local centre for the unemployed, or just a friend. Of course if there are guidelines to operate by and there is real evidence to justify disqualification, then these should only ensure that the procedure is seen to be fair. In fact appeals where the full range of advisers are present are far more likely to end up in the appellant's favour than those that are determined in private. The decision will still be taken by the same person, who will still be the only person to see the 'evidence', but something seems to change. As usual, we are not to be allowed to know.

The secret evidence culture also helps to keep people quiet when they're visited by the outdoor investigation unit. Since you don't know what they believe about you, you won't be too keen to cause trouble. It's only when they keep you waiting in the rain and examine your fingernails to see if there is mud on them, or ask you how you can afford a fur coat if you're unemployed, that people get sufficiently annoyed to complain.

Much the same thing happens to the most maligned of all those in receipt of welfare, the sick. This group have been the target of the media heavy gang for years. Statistics about the number who don't come when summoned to a medical referee examination are presumed to prove wholesale fiddling, when it might just prove that people were sick temporarily and went back to work. And each person on disability benefit has to have a *weekly* doctor's certificate confirming that they are not fit for work. Even superficial examination of the scheme should—but won't—dilute a lot of the criticism.

If you're sick and want to claim disability benefit you have to be so certified by a doctor. You have between one chance in three and one chance in four of being summoned for examination by a medical referee. This referee operates in premises and with facilities provided by the Department of Social Welfare and is an employee of the department. The department has refused on numerous occasions to let me know the equipment that is provided in these premises, other than to say that they are 'adequate' to do the job. It is presumably therefore a state secret.

The medical referee acts entirely on his or her own and is not obliged to discuss the matter with the claimant's GP nor indeed with the specialist where one is involved (though the specialist may if he or she wishes complete a form for the medical referee). They are deemed competent to, and frequently do, overrule not just a GP but a specialist too. They are not obliged to give reasons. Where the decision goes against the claimant he or she simply gets a standard form that says they have been found fit for work. This can be, and frequently is, done without access to the claimant's medical records, not to mention discussion with other doctors (unless a GP or specialist is prepared to accompany the claimant to the examination or fill in the form). The referees are not obliged to supply any evidence or argument to sustain the conclusion they come to, unless the disqualified person seeks it. Neither will they discuss the matter with the claimant's doctor after the decision.

I (and I'm sure every present or previous member of the Oireachtas) have met people who have collapsed on their way in or out of medical referee examinations and still been pronounced fit to work. I know of doctors informing patients that they would no longer be responsible for them if they went back to work, because the medical referee said they had to. I know of cases where the diagnosis of specialist consultants has been overruled in these examinations. But no-one can argue, because the decision is final. Any appeal is within the department. If there really is a difference of opinion between two equally competent and conscientious doctors then the decision about who is right should be taken by a competent medical practitioner, not a civil servant.

The Department of Social Welfare duck all the questions about secrecy and accountability that arise here and instead tell us that the scheme has been particularly good at eliminating abuse. They are actually quite proud of their achievements! Given that, it's strange that they don't follow it through to the logical conclusion. Each disqualified claimant had been certified as unfit to work by a doctor, in circumstances where the department decides the person isn't sick at all. There must be a lot of crooked or incompetent doctors in practice if the department is right. (And let us remember that the department is quite happy to suggest that the medical referee scheme is particularly good at eliminating fraud, thereby branding those who are disqualified as 'frauds'.)

Surely in the interest of the general public as well as the department these should be reported to the Irish Medical Council. Perhaps they will be some time, but up to now they've reported none. I spent a lot of time wondering why. The elimination of rogue doctors would be in everyone's interests after all, and would reduce the pressure on the majority of doctors to certify people under dubious circumstances. The department would obviously benefit too. But of course there is a problem. The Medical Council, inconveniently, wouldn't take the word of the department about these doctors. It would insist on looking at the evidence on which the complaint was based. It would look at the records of the 'offending' doctor, and probably talk to the patient as well. But natural justice, and the prospect of a High Court action, would mean that the Medical Council would insist on adjudicating on the diagnoses of the medical referee as well. This would involve an assessment of their notes and of the equipment available to them.

The department is not averse to suggesting that certain doctors are very liberal in the dispensing of medical certificates, clearly implying that their referee system is adept at catching these 'offenders'. But naming such offenders would be another matter entirely! And all this could end up in the High Court. The barrier of secrecy would be well and truly breached. But silence is safer, and so no doctors are reported.

Secrecy is not confined to the operations of central government when it comes to dealing with the poor. The final recourse of all poor people is to the Community Welfare Officer, who administers the Supplementary Welfare Scheme. This scheme, which is operated by the health boards but financed directly by the Department of Social Welfare, is designed to ensure that no-one goes without the basics of food, shelter, heat and light because of poverty. It provides a minimum income and rent support, and can provide fuel, clothing, and other supports. Theoretically decisions are made by the individual officers, and they are free to exercise their discretion. Nevertheless there is a remarkable consistency about the way the scheme operates around the country. Most people will only get assistance with an ESB bill once, and will only get support to pay a deposit for a flat once. Clothing allowances will be paid around the country in a remarkably consistent fashion, even though individual officers are supposed to exercise their discretion in individual cases. There is a procedure for appeals too when you are refused a payment. No-one is too clear how the appeal system works, and there was a suspicion that the appeal was adjudicated on by the same officer who had refused the claim!

Clearly there are regulations and guidelines that produce these uniform practices and result in similar appeals procedures too. But we don't know. And the evidence on which a claim is refused or reduced is also, typically, not available.

The obsession with secrecy is most painful obviously for those who are in need of the support of the state for survival. They are at the receiving end in a personal and often humiliating way. But others feel it too. All the voluntary organisations are aware of their own exclusion from both information and policy-making. Groups working with the homeless pursue a fruitless campaign to get the Department of the Environment to make a proper assessment of the numbers of the homeless; groups working with the young homeless have similar problems. And all the organisations dealing with all our social problems have one common experience. They are told regularly, both by politicians and bureaucrats, how important their contribution is. They are offered much rhetorical encouragement and an increasing level of physical and resource support. But they are kept firmly on the outside when it comes to policy-making. They are, like those they attempt to assist, 'recipients'. They are told little, asked little, and unaware of any major influence on policy. Only a culture of openness, transparency and accountability could change that.

7 Trust Me, I Know What I'm Doing

● ●

We have looked at so much that it's difficult to believe there is much more the state can keep secret. But there is more, so much more that this chapter is only a sampler. It does illustrate fairly well the instincts of the system.

Lots of excuses are put forward, but most can be safely categorised under two headings. Documents are withheld from publication either because, we are told, it is not the practice to disclose such information or because it is not in the public interest. This might be for reasons of national security or for less specific reasons. Seán Doherty justified his by now famous phone tapping on the grounds of national security, after all, so that is clearly capable of a broad interpretation. The 'public interest' reason is usually the one that arises, ironically enough, when material is withheld in which the public has a great interest! One way or the other, though, the instinct is always towards secrecy.

We are only aware of these attitudes when we at least become aware of the existence of documents or information. Much more is probably even more securely suppressed, because we don't even know enough to ask about it. Mary Robinson highlighted this during the Seanad debate on my Freedom of Information Bill in 1988. She outlined a case involving the refusal of a fuel allowance to a woman. The woman had courageously gone to court, and the final, late defence offered by the state was that she was ineligible under guidelines issued by the relevant minister. The existence of these guidelines was unknown until the state entered its defence, and they were subsequently found by the courts to be illegal. God alone knows how many other sets of secret guidelines, of perhaps dubious legality, are floating around Government departments and state agencies. You could try your luck in court, but you might not succeed, as another case outlined by Mary Robinson suggests. This again involved, perhaps inevitably, the Department of Social Welfare. In this case a person sought the support of the courts and claimed that the department had not operated fairly in his case. This was supported by a sworn affidavit from a senior official of the National Social Services Board explaining the procedure for granting the particular benefit and explaining how the appellant was qualified to receive it. The department replied that the NSSB official wasn't quite right; their procedure was different, but they declined to say exactly how! The irony is compounded by the fact that it is the NSSB that advises Citizens' Advice Bureaus throughout the country. Advice in the dark is obviously the department's policy!

I first ran into the instinct for secrecy early in my political career. I was fortuitously selected to be a member of a parliamentary delegation travelling to an inter-parliamentary conference in Cuba—a piece of good fortune that befell me less than a week after I was first elected to the Seanad. Shortly before I left I was provided with what was described as 'confidential' briefing material from the Department of Foreign Affairs. The confidentiality was heavily emphasised to me, perhaps because I was new and 'unreliable'. I devoured the material, eagerly assuming that I was privy to the entire accumulated wisdom of the department on Cuba and on the issues that were to arise at the conference. I found instead a collection of bland clichés and information that was already familiar to me from a reasonably informed interest in current affairs. What was perhaps most informative was the selectivity of the information. Cuba clearly had few good points and emerged very much in colours that the US State Department would have approved of. It was clear which 'side' we were on. My scepticism was confirmed when I discovered that one of the key documents in my high-level briefing was a photocopy of a review article from the *Harvard Business Review* on the state of the Cuban economy. This article, which I still have, was, as might be expected considering the source, not very complimentary. The catalogue of negatives was almost complete when the author addressed the question of why, if the economy was so awful, Castro was apparently still popular. This was attributed to the quality of the health, educational, sporting and other facilities available to the Cuban people! The intriguing question of how a failed economy managed to provide such excellent services was of course not considered at all.

Nevertheless, all this material, even though it was either available from the news media or consisted of photocopies of foreign journals, was meant to be secret! Apparently it's secret even if it's published.

Of course the briefing material, while of virtually no use as a briefing on Cuba, was a remarkable insight into attitudes in the Department of Foreign Affairs. Perhaps that was why they had no desire to have the material published! Indeed that department has always struggled to avoid any semblance of public accountability for its day-to-day operations. It is the only department, for instance, that ever to my knowledge contacted a member of the Oireachtas directly and asked that a motion be withdrawn. Attitudes there are probably best summed up by my own experience during a debate in the Seanad on the case of the Birmingham Six. I outlined the well-documented obstructionism of the Irish embassy in Washington in the early days of that campaign, and suggested that it was time the Government gave up such tactics, moved beyond expressing concern about the case and actually said that they thought the Six were innocent. Those remarks were described both in the Seanad and outside by the then junior minister, George Bermingham, as 'amongst the most irresponsible' he'd ever heard! How little they are prepared to trust us! How much they believe they know better than us!

But secretive attitudes are not confined to Government departments: they also pervade the houses of the Oireachtas themselves. Even there appears to be a determination to ensure that democratic accountability will be minimal. This attitude is well illustrated by the second of what I can call my formative experiences. This relates to the infamous officially unpublished book known as 'Rulings of the Chair', within which are documented all the precedent-setting decisions of both the Cathaoirleach of the Seanad and the Ceann Comhairle. It is by reference to these decisions that these officers make rulings and decisions about what is and isn't admissible, in order, urgent, and the like, for the purposes of business in the Dáil and Seanad. An outsider would think that reference to it would enable members to ensure that they were operating within the rules at all times. Dr John O'Connell, when he was Ceann Comhairle, thought so too, and proposed to give each member a copy. That was twelve years ago, and it still hasn't happened. Knowledge is power, after all, and who knows better than the bureaucrat! It should come as no surprise then to learn that the meetings of the Committee of Procedures and Privileges of both the Dáil and Seanad—the defenders of the rights and privileges of members—are private; so are their minutes and records.

The dealings of the bureaucracy with the houses of the Oireachtas illustrate this point further. I was a member of the Joint Committee on Irish, and suggested that since we had no money we should seek submissions from the citizens of the Gaeltacht by way of a letter to the local papers in each area. I was told that we'd need permission for that, though I could never establish who it was precisely that was required to give a committee of the Oireachtas permission to write a letter. The purveyor of permissions was overruled on that occasion, but the attitude was eloquent.

Irish was not the only victim of bureaucratic and Government secretiveness. The Dáil Committee on Public Expenditure not long ago noticed that the Department of Justice had spent over ten million pounds on planning prisons that were never built. They were invited to explain this to the committee, but declined, on the instructions of the then minister, Gerry Collins. National security, the great excuse, was cited.

The determination to ensure that such committees are kept firmly in check is underlined by the skimpy funding that has always been provided. When I was a member of the Seanad the total budget for all committees would have amounted to less than the travel budget of the Department of Finance. Executive and bureaucracy worked smoothly together to prevent any notion of accountability or independent thinking taking hold.

But it's not just from members of the Oireachtas that the system withholds information. It is even more cavalier with the public in general. Studies are prepared and reports commissioned, all paid for by the taxpayer, but the taxpayer isn't allowed to see them—all in the public interest, of course! Significant examples of this are the study on the operation of building societies carried out by the predecessor to the Director of Consumer Affairs. Mortgage holders would have been intrigued to find out what these arrogant and indifferent organisations were really like. They are not to know, unfortunately: it would not be 'in the public interest'. As usual, nobody bothered to ask the poor old public.

Then they moved on to Social Welfare. In the middle 1980s yet another of the 'welfare fraud' flurries hit the headlines, and Michael Woods, never one to miss a publicity opportunity, commissioned an international firm of consultants to investigate. They did, and confirmed that fraud was of close to negligible proportions—or at least a skimpy summary of their report said so. The full report, needless to say, was never published. The justification was that proposals to combat fraud were contained in the full report and could not be published. In a more open society the report would have been written in such a way that recommendations on avoiding fraud could have been kept secret while the details of the department's competence or otherwise would have been made known to the public, who after all, and it bears repeating, are paying for the department.

But I suppose from what we already know about Social Welfare the surprise would have been if they had published the report. We might, though, have expected better from less byzantine departments, particularly those that were responsible for the health and welfare of the public. Yet when we had poisoned cucumbers on the market and the state identified the source—an irresponsible grower using prohibited pesticides—it was decided that the name of the offender couldn't be made public 'for legal reasons'. It's the same when rivers are polluted.

Remember all the fish kills we have had over the years. In how many of those cases was there ever a prosecution in which the dumpers of toxic material were identified and punished? In Cork the River Lee turns green if there is a dry spell during the summer. Which farmers are using excessive amounts of fertilisers? Nobody is prepared to say. Scepticism about the official position is added to when you realise that the local authorities, with their vast resources, are only responsible for a small number of the pollution-related prosecutions that take place. The majority are pursued by the fisheries boards, operating with a tiny fraction of the local authorities' resources.

Governments are wary too of reports that point to deficiencies in Government policy and can always find reasons not to publish them. Among the most bizarre examples of this was the decision not to publish the report of the task force set up some years age to suggest a programme of revitalisation for Cork. The task force reported to the Government; the Government published its response to the report but refused to publish the report! It was hardly a national security matter, so one must conclude that the traditional and understandable Cork preoccupation with centralisation was expressed fairly bluntly in the report. That this was the cause of refusal to publish would of course be denied. Instead it would be suggested that the report might contain commercially sensitive information and hence could not be published.

Other Government departments make it clear that the secrecy obsession is universal and not just the product of an individual department's eccentricities. Not so long ago the Government set up a review body on the Defence Forces. This was a response to the protests of army wives against the pay and conditions of members. Action by the wives was necessary because it was illegal for their husbands to form any kind of an organisation to negotiate about and publicise their pay grievances. The logic was clear from all that. Secrecy and powerlessness are tools of government. Because they were refused rights the rest of us took for granted, and notwithstanding the colourful torrents of rhetorical praise, the Defence Forces were paid badly because it was easy to ignore them, because they had no rights.

Secrecy has always been the option when the going gets tough. It is difficult now to believe that until 1992 reports by the Department of the Marine and its predecessors on accidents at sea were kept secret, ostensibly to ensure that witnesses spoke freely to the investigators! Extend that thinking to the courts and we wouldn't have much of a criminal justice system. We would have investigation in secret, followed by trial in secret, followed by locking away of the evidence (which, come to think of it, resembles the operations of An Bord Pleanála quite closely).

But the reticence doesn't just extend to marine accidents: it appears to extend to industrial accidents generally, and indeed to inspections carried out in the interest of safety and to ensure that minimum standards prevail in working environments. One could understand a degree of reticence in a situation where a legal case was pending or where a possibility of contempt of court proceedings existed. Unfortunately the system thinks in broader terms than that. I was in contact some years ago with a worker who complained that her work-place was too cold and who sought an inspection by the then Factory Inspectorate. The worker felt that the inspection that she believes was carried out was carried out incorrectly. So her solicitor wrote to the Factory Inspectorate seeking a copy of the inspector's report. The reply from the factory inspector, which is in my possession, first of all does not confirm that the inspection took place at all, and then goes on to say that the 'results of any inspection ... are confidential to the Minister ...' One can just imagine the then Minister for Labour, Bertie Ahern, resolutely retaining for himself details of how cold or how hot it was in a provincial food-processing factory.

In the culture of secrecy the instinct is always to refuse information, except where compelled to release it. This has the convenient side-effect of reducing the potential for ministerial and bureaucratic embarrassment. A recent study on the school transport system requested by Séamus Brennan when he was Minister for Education was only published after a long delay. No reason was given for this.

It comes as no surprise then to find almost identical assertions of a duty of confidentiality in the legislation setting up new state agencies. In each case a leak of confidential information is made a criminal offence, and the definition of what is confidential information is left to the agency itself. There are no guidelines, no broad bands of information, no exclusions for malpractice or indeed the public interest. Confidentiality is absolute, and the criminal law will enforce it. We find ourselves in a situation where bodies like FÁS spend vast quantities of public money but operate primarily according to the rules of the private sector, deciding major policy shifts without any public access to their decision-making structures. Why does it sound so subversive to suggest that the minutes of board meetings of bodies like FÁS should be open to the public, that discussion papers put to that board by its management should be similarly publicly accessible, and that the board should meet in public except where there is a clear *a priori* need for secrecy? As we'll see, this is what happens elsewhere, and the world didn't fall down, though some bureaucrats did! Imagine what it would be like if the records of all the secret meetings of the multiplicity of 'quangos' were to become public property! Utopian and impracticable, we'll be told. But it happens elsewhere, and it works.

8 RICH, POWERFUL, SECRET, AND GREEDY

● ●

O ne of the little irritations of life is the need many people
seem to have to keep on reminding us that we live in a
market economy. There can often be an added tone to
these assertions that reminds us how lucky we are that life is as
so described. In case we're not as sure as our betters about this,
we are reminded further that what we are living in is a 'free'
market economy. Indeed for many of those dedicated souls in
what is called the '*free*' press the words 'freedom' and 'market'
are virtually synonymous. 'You can't', as Albert Reynolds might
say, 'have one without the other.'

As with so much else, little analysis follows the assertion. A
market economy is assumed to envelop us and—rather like the
famous uncertainty principle in physics—we can't analyse it, we
can only assume its existence. Or so it seems from the vagueness
of most of what our commentators offer to us by way of
explanation. We are fed a wholesome dose of financial clichés
and rhetoric. We know too about the rights of property,
enshrined in the Constitution. But that's it really. 'Free' markets,
the rights of property and vague words like 'competition',
'enterprise' and, more recently, 'choice' are to be our lot. And
since all this is clearly a good thing, we are encouraged to lie
back and enjoy it.

One of my favourite one-liners is attributed to Harold
Macmillan, who said late on in life: 'Whenever I find that the

establishment are unanimous about anything they are almost invariably wrong.' So the market economy unanimity set me thinking and reading about it. I learnt about the theory of the market economy, which was based on the assumption of perfect competition, competition being, it appears, the ultimate 'good thing' in the non-carnal sense of those words. This perfect competition presumed that there would be so many people providing goods and services that we would have endless choice, and no one supplier could push the consumer around. From the consumer's point of view it sounded even better when I read that perfect competition was also supposed to mean that the customer had all the knowledge he or she could possibly need in order to make a rational choice about how to dispose of his or her money. It was a vision of utopia: diligent entrepreneurs titillating every need of the perfectly informed consumer.

Now I realised that if you didn't have money there might be problems, and I wondered about the price an employee of all these wonderful entrepreneurs would pay in this frenetic competitive world. I even wondered about who precisely the consumer was going to be, and how he or she was going to have time and/or money to enjoy the myriad goods and services. It seemed to me that they might all be too poor and too exhausted and too busy at work to bother with all these products of their long hours, low wages, and frenetic competition. I was having great difficulty finding anything more than the vaguest similarity between the utopian theory and the reality of life in Ireland.

Then I had a flash of inspiration. I realised that many of the things that annoyed people were the sort of thing I've described in earlier chapters relating to services provided by the state. And I knew that in most of those areas there was no real competition. Clearly they would not be an appropriate test of the match between the theory and reality. They would be unresponsive, secretive, much as I've described them. My search for examples of the functioning 'free' market economy should focus on the private sector. And so I looked. I searched for the information that would help me to understand how the market economy worked. I knew enough to ignore advertising and company publicity: I was looking for real information. Advertising and company PR were designed to persuade people to make decisions: they were clearly going to be loaded. I wanted to find out how it was that a citizen-consumer was going to find out solid factual information about a company and its products.

Were they safe, for instance? Had they been tested recently by Eolas or another state body? Had any products been found to be more safety-conscious than others? I knew that the Director of Consumer Affairs could force dangerous goods to be withdrawn from the market; and I knew that all goods manufactured or sold within the European Union must be certified by their manufacturers as meeting appropriate safety and other standards, standards that are reasonable but not excessive.

What the consumer would be interested in, though, would not be minimum standards alone but rather the best value in terms of safety, reliability, and durability. This information is what enables you to get good value for money, after all. Information like that is the essence of the competitive, free-market economy.

Tests obviously are done, since goods are regularly withdrawn from the market if they are found to be unsafe, usually by a state agency but occasionally by responsible manufacturers. The tests involve assessing the compliance of goods with regulations and standards, and must show the extent to which different products exceed or presumably don't meet those standards. Consumers would love to get their hands on those test results, and one would imagine that publication would clearly stimulate competition, that great objective of national and EU policy. Consumers in Ireland will be disappointed. Just as it is with nursing homes, as it has been with the industrial inspectorate, so is it with consumer goods in general. All test results that do not show that goods are unsafe are 'confidential'. Can they really assess safety without assessing reliability, durability, performance, and so on? Of course they can't! So clearly the information is assembled, but the person in whose name it is assembled, the consumer, will remain in ignorance. Commercial confidentiality, we will be told, is the reason. The consequence of all this is that bodies like the Consumers' Associations must, at considerable expense, duplicate many of these tests for the benefit of their members.

State agencies frequently use arguments about fairness to

justify their reticence. Since not all televisions, nursing homes or toys are tested, it would be unfair to all those who were not tested if they had to compete with those who had been tested and been shown to be good value. Possible legal action is usually mentioned. Nevertheless small and poorly financed consumer bodies do try to conduct such tests, and they survive. Is the state really so vulnerable?

We can only conclude that there are reasons other than those stated for the silence. It seems to me to relate clearly to the way the market operates. In fact the market works too well for the comfort of its proponents. This is because consumers, when they get access to information, take appropriate action. Classic examples are where people are alerted to possible health risks associated with a particular cheese, or where there is a salmonella scare. Consumer resistance produces a quick clearing-out of suspect products, an example of the 'free' market working as it should to guarantee product quality. This is usually followed first by howls of complaint from suppliers of the now suspect product and a little later by reassuring noises from the appropriate minister trying to persuade us to start buying again!

It comes as no shock, then, to discover that manufacturers have been campaigning vigorously, and with hopes of some success, it appears, to undermine one of the most pro-consumer regulations we have, one that has produced dramatic changes in consumer habits. This is the requirement that all ingredients be listed on the packaging of foodstuffs. 'E numbers' have become such a deterrent to purchase that a vigorous lobby is seeking to have the regulations changed to remove specific reference to the numbers and replace it with a bland reference to 'permitted preservatives, colourings, etc.'

The first conclusion we reach about the market economy must be that we are a long way still from its realisation. Well-informed market participants are, it appears, bad for the market economy, though I couldn't find any reference to that in the theory!

The 'free' market isn't supposed to apply just to consumer goods and food, though. It is also supposed to apply in the area of business generally. It's supposed to apply to the financial markets, to the property market, to the market in land, and to the operation of the stock market.

Clearly anyone buying a new house would like to know as much as possible about the builder who's selling the property. Similarly a person thinking about investing in a publicly quoted company, that is, a company whose shares are bought and sold on the Stock Exchange, would wish to know as much as possible about the company. The need becomes even more urgent since the company is most probably a limited liability company, that is, a company in which the total liabilities of its directors cannot exceed the initial sums put into it by them. That clearly is an enormous privilege and is presumably designed to encourage 'enterprise', another of those magic words. The idea is that people can undertake new business ventures, and if the venture goes wrong then only the money invested in the company can be lost. This obviously will be a matter of some concern to people and institutions who supply either loans or credit to the company. They would like to be sure that they weren't taking excessive risks. They would like to know as much as possible about the background of the company.

People will choose their own indicators in a situation like this. Some will be interested in the existing debts of the company. Others will be interested in the existence of any outstanding tax liabilities by the company. This is because the Revenue Commissioners come before everyone else in the queue when debts are to be repaid. For others the names of the individuals behind the company will be a useful indicator. The previous business record of a person can presumably be a good predictor of future behaviour. A prudent business person will be slow to extend either loans or credit to a company whose directors have a string of collapsed companies in their history.

Then there are people who believe that it's well worth while finding out how generously the directors of a company reward themselves. They like to know precisely how much the directors have so far taken out of a company. It's also important information if you are a shareholder and are wondering why your dividends aren't bigger. A breakdown of directors' fees would be useful information.

All this information and more might well be useful, but you won't get much of it. First of all it is often impossible to sort out who exactly is the beneficial owner of a company, even more so if that company is not listed on the Stock Exchange—and only a small minority are. The beneficial owner is the person or people to whom any money made by the company will finally be delivered. Companies not involved in the stock market are private companies. Many such companies have directors who are nominees, which means they are no more than a front for people who don't wish to be identified. Elaborate networks of interlinked companies are created in this way, so elaborate that even the most experienced corporate lawyer or accountant will fail to penetrate them. Indeed even the state often has difficulty here, something that is well illustrated by recent events in the cattle industry and by the now well-reported story of Telecom Éireann's purchase of the Johnston, Mooney and O'Brien site in Dublin. In the case of the beef industry the Fair Trade Tribunal, at the instigation of the Department of Industry and Commerce, was forced some years ago to spend large sums of money finding out who owned a particular segment of the beef industry. The department evidently believed that Larry Goodman was the beneficial owner, but Mr Goodman denied it. There was apparently no simple way of settling this. The investigation concluded that Mr Goodman was the owner, but even then he resolutely denied it. Newspaper reports suggested, however, that it was listed as a Goodman Group asset when Mr Goodman had his little crisis some years later.

Things hadn't changed much a few years later when the Government again spent hundreds of thousands of pounds finding out who really owned a mysterious company that made a lot of money out of the Telecom Éireann land purchase. The investigation concluded that Dermot Desmond had a beneficial interest in it, which, again, he promptly denied.

You would conclude from all this that company law is vague and imprecise. It is not. Company law is among the most complex there is, exceeding even the Finance Acts. I can vouch for this from personal experience, having been involved, in the Seanad, for what seemed to be endless hours of detailed discussion and amendment to one of the most recent Companies Bills. This was an unbelievably detailed bill listing, among other things, the conditions under which companies could be set up, regulating the relationship between companies and their directors, limiting the loans that companies could give to directors, and so on. One of its well-publicised objectives was to deal with what had become known as the 'phoenix syndrome'. This was the activity, familiar to many house purchasers, whereby unscrupulous building companies went into liquidation, leaving estates unfinished, and the directors of the apparently insolvent company surfaced quite quickly in a new company but with all their debts attached to the failed company. Many procedures were listed in the Companies Bill to prevent this happening, and many of them were no doubt well intentioned.

I was always intrigued, however, by how protective it was of any possibility of disclosure of information on identified individuals. Indeed a certain mystique seemed to cover the state's perception of the 'daring young men' who set up companies for whatever purpose. The mystique was clearly evident in the resistance the Government showed to the idea of treating 'insider trading' as a criminal offence. 'Insider trading' involves people who have access to secret information, for instance early warning of a firm's trading results or oil exploration results, buying or selling shares before everyone else has the information. Fortunes can be, were and are being made in this way, as my former colleague and long-time stockbroker Senator Shane Ross assures me. The clear wish of the Government was that the matter would be dealt with by the Stock Exchange rather than by the criminal law. Leaving the Stock Exchange to deal with these abuses would be a bit like leaving the bookies to regulate the betting industry. It took huge public pressure to persuade the Government to agree to make such thievery a criminal offence.

Attitudes to 'insider trading' epitomised both that bill and the law as it finally emerged. Nowhere is it clear that the customers of a company or even the state have a right to know who exactly are the beneficial owners of a company. Clearly this would not be a difficult section to draft, involving as it would a simple obligation to identify the individuals who stood to gain from the transactions of a company. And it's worth remembering that 'gains' from a company can include artificial losses that offset taxes elsewhere. Nevertheless, successive Governments have resisted any such simplification. Ireland has also consistently attempted to frustrate EU attempts to increase the amount of information that companies must disclose. Recent exercises involved persuading the EU to require only very limited disclosure by what were described as 'small' companies. It subsequently emerged that the vast majority of the Irish work force was employed in such 'small' enterprises. Secrecy was safely sustained. Indeed the amount of information that employees are entitled to receive about their employers is minimal too. It's even difficult to find out if tax and PRSI deductions have been forwarded to the Revenue Commissioners.

If the Government can't find out who owns something and obviously doesn't want to give itself powers to do so, then clearly the unfortunate small trader or creditor will have even less knowledge. Nevertheless, as we saw, information and its availability is central to the functioning of the 'free' market economy we are expected to enjoy. It is interesting to note in this regard what *Business Age*, described as Britain's best-selling business magazine, had to say in its autumn 1993 issue:

'One of the problems with evaluating Irish-based wealth is the lack of figures. Most Irish enterprises are family-run and privately controlled. Disclosure rules are minimal.'

A quick look at the 'top 500' listed by the *Sunday Business Post* on 30 January 1994 confirms that view, with almost 75 per cent of Ireland's top 500 companies disclosing no profit (or loss) figures! This of course leaves customers and employees at a disadvantage, a fact recognised by the far more stringent disclosure regulations in other countries. One can only conclude that in Ireland the privacy of the rich and powerful is more important to the Government than the efficient functioning of the market economy. Disclosure rules are far more demanding in the United States, and shareholders demand and are given details both of directors' remuneration and of company policy with regard to environmental and other matters.

Even if you are able to find out who precisely the owners or main shareholders of a company are, you will still find information hard to come by. Try finding out the exact details of the share options held by individual directors, for instance, or the fees paid to directors. Try getting an AGM of a publicly quoted company to seek more detailed information from its directors. You could even try to find out the company's environmental policy, or its wage policy, or its attitudes to trade unions, and you will discover what silence can really mean. You will also discover that while large numbers of individual shareholders will support you, any votes will go overwhelmingly against you. We will see later on why that tends to be the case.

Building societies are theoretically much less nasty beasts than companies, whether private or public. They are meant to be mutual societies set up by their members for the benefit of the members. It would be reasonable to expect, therefore, that you would be told why you were refused a mortgage, for instance. A case I'm familiar with illustrates many people's experience. A mortgage holder moved from one part of Ireland to the other, sold his old house, found a new one, and then sought and was granted a mortgage. He completed the direct debit form as requested, and then noticed that no money was being removed from his account. He questioned this twice in a period of nine months, but no precise information was forthcoming. It came later, though, in the form of a letter saying that the building society was seeking repossession on the grounds of non-payment of the mortgage. He protested, but they persisted. He was told that he should have brought the repayments into the building society.

After much fuss and before the court case, it emerged that the building society had made a mistake, and so the court case never materialised. The victim paid up his 'arrears' and carried on. He then received a bill seeking extra interest on the arrears, even though the arrears were admitted to be the fault of the building society. He refused to pay. Then he moved to another town and sold his house. The building society withheld the extra interest from his cheque. He fumed and carried on, lodging the net proceeds of his house sale in a different building society. The new building society refused him a mortgage. No reason was given, but the case is clear evidence of a network of information that is both secret and probably illegal under the Data Protection Act.

Even though my acquaintance eventually got a mortgage elsewhere, his experience would make a building society member wary of those to whom they had entrusted their savings. It would at the very least encourage you to seek more information about 'your' building society. You might like to find how much the directors of the society pay themselves. It would be reassuring to believe that they kept a tight rein on such things, particularly since it turned out that one senior executive of a building society didn't think that £50,000 commission from an insurance company to himself was significant enough to mention even to his fellow-directors.

That sort of thing, coupled with the controversy surrounding Edmund Farrell at the Irish Permanent Building Society, provoked a flurry of 'openness' from the Irish Permanent and others. Though there was a considerable (and presumably expensive) fuss made at the time about all this, the full extent of this 'openness' is clear from an *Irish Times* report of 29 July 1993. The Irish Permanent announced that it will be run on 'principles of openness, integrity, and accountability'. A new code of practice was introduced, we were told, that stated that customers should be given details of any fees and charges levied on them in addition to normal loan repayments. In other words, it appears that if the society now wants to take any extra money from us, they have voluntarily and in their own eyes magnanimously agreed to tell us about it. I'm still not clear what exactly they used to do before they introduced the code! It was nevertheless reassuring to note that the practice of conducting society business with directors' firms 'has now ceased'. It went out with a bang, though, with £630,000 being paid in 1992 to firms associated with non-executive directors.

Clearly all this was traumatic for the poor directors, because they resolutely refused any further disclosures. Details of payments to executives 'will remain secret.' Aggregate figures will continue to be made known, but not who gets what. Equal resolution was shown in refusing to disclose the 'amounts of commission payments it receives from insurance companies.' 'Market practice' was the justification for the secrecy in those two cases. It's difficult to see what market practice it was that prevented the directors of the Irish Permanent from telling their own members how much it cost to publish and circulate 400,000 copies of the 'openness' code in a colour brochure.

Let us remind ourselves once again that the Irish Permanent Building Society, contrary to appearances, was not a private family company. It was a mutual society that was theoretically owned by the members, that is, people who have a certain kind of savings with them or who have mortgages with them. It says something for our institutional order that it was only when the Irish Permanent decided to move from its mutual status and seek to become a public limited company with a stock market flotation that the secrecy was, at least temporarily, suspended. Then we discovered that the chief executive earned up to £300,000 a year. The chairman (part-time) was paid £80,000 a year, and non-executive directors (even more part-time!) were paid £20,000 a year. Perhaps their previous reticence is understandable!

Responsibility for the Irish Permanent and other building societies was transferred in recent years to the Central Bank, in order, presumably, to reassure us that all was well with our savings. The Central Bank has considerable powers to seek information from the various companies for which it is responsible. The companies must also supply considerable information to the Central Bank about such matters as preferential loans to directors. But only a limited amount of the information supplied to the Central Bank is made known. We know even less about the information the bank seeks of its own volition. So it looks as if we're back to the secretive 'trust me, I know what I'm doing' approach that characterises the state and its agencies. But then what better symbol is there of centralised secretiveness than the Department of Finance; and of course former secretaries of that department almost inevitably end up as governors of the Central Bank.

Nevertheless the Central Bank has a job to do. It regulates the banks as well as the building societies and is presumably therefore the final regulator of what the Irish Permanent Building Society refers to as 'market practice'. It could enforce disclosure on banks and building societies, but it doesn't. It presumably sees its job as custodian of the security of the institutions, not protector of the customers nor even encourager of competition in a 'free', well-informed market economy.

Which brings us back to the question of why you'll never extract more than the minimum of information at the AGM of a public company. That's because the majority of the shares are usually held or controlled either by directors or by institutions like banks, pension funds, and insurance companies. Obviously they don't want to set any information bandwagon going, since they themselves would be the first to be hauled on board. Silence is therefore preferred. For the banks and other institutional investors this is meant to convey a sense of being somewhat above all the nastiness of the market. They are, after all, almost national institutions. And they usually get away with that in their collective identity. Individual customers know differently! Far from being detached and superior, the financial institutions engage in lobbying of an intensity that, because it is rarely mentioned, is not at all appreciated. At least I've rarely read about it and wouldn't know about it had I not been at the receiving end. Even obscure and easily forgotten independent senators were apparently to be influenced if at all possible. What other reason could there be for both the then chairman of Allied Irish Banks, Niall Crowley, and later the then governor of the Bank of Ireland, Louden Ryan, inviting me to lunch in their offices immediately after I had had some particularly rude thing to say about both major banks? They hardly invited me along to discuss social justice.

The reaction of the average citizen to all this may well be that 'the banks are a rotten shower, but so what?' And if the financial institutions were no more than ordinary businesses attempting to influence policy by lobbying, the average citizen would be right. Unfortunately they are much worse than that. In the first place any major financial institution is in a position to undermine the currency if they don't like Government policy. This can be, and has been, done simply by moving money into other countries. They deny that, of course, and speak instead of 'market forces', as if such forces were as incomprehensible and independent of human control as the weather. The truth is that money doesn't 'flow' from one country to another, it is sent, and it's sent when bankers and others don't like what a government is doing. So national governments end up competing to see who can keep the bankers happy, which of course makes the bankers very happy and also very powerful. And they don't hesitate to use that power.

That ruthlessness was very clear in the early days of Alan Dukes's period as Minister for Finance. Mr Dukes had spotted a tax avoidance device known as 'bond-washing', which enabled people in the know to avoid paying large amounts of income tax. He announced his intention of ending it, and the financial institutions were not amused. They launched an attack that involved a concerted attempt to sell off Government stock to the value of two billion pounds in a couple of days. If it had succeeded the Government would have been bankrupt. Far less threatening displays of power by trade unions have provoked outrage; but in this case we are not even to know who did it, or how they were persuaded not to see it through.

So a funny market economy it is. You are not to know what the Government may know about the goods you buy in the shops. At the same time the Government works resolutely to ensure that neither the ordinary individual nor indeed the Government itself will find out much about those who, through their wealth and the power it brings, can devastate all our lives. Cynics would say that we are in a 'free' market all right, but one that is somewhat different from that beloved of economists. Our 'free market' is one in which ordinary people can be 'freely' bought and sold by individuals who are neither accountable or known to them, who use information we are not allowed to see, and who can reward themselves at our expense without telling us about it.

9 THE DATA PROTECTION ACT

• •

O ur masters are not just diligent keepers of secrets: they are also diligent gatherers of information. They gather it about us from the moment we are born, and one could hardly argue with that. Information about births and about infant health and mortality are obviously of great assistance in planning natal and neonatal facilities, for instance. For years much of that information and information assembled throughout our lives, other than that supplied to the Registrar of Births, Marriages, and Deaths, was hardly accessible at all, being buried in obscure filing cabinets somewhere. Large-scale breaches of privacy were unthinkable, because of the volume of tedious manual work that would first be required. Files were often hard to come by: only a genuine concern for the security of the state or the well-being of the individual would have overcome the inertia that beset most public bodies when it came to searching for information. People who had to deal with the Department of Social Welfare, in particular, were acutely aware of the mysterious 'flying file' that, when it wasn't in transit between Dublin and wherever the applicant lived, was in a state of apparent suspended animation between two different offices of that same department. Often, it appeared, only a question in the Dáil had the power to 'rematerialise' it.

Computers eventually changed all that, even in the Department of Social Welfare. They brought with them both greater efficiency and a dramatically easier way of gaining access to data. This was at first seen to be a good thing. It could make for a more efficient service to the public and also enable large organisations to handle their data more efficiently. In many countries, though, both civil libertarians and more civilised governments began to see the dangers. Large-scale computers linked together could enable both the state and private groups to pry into everything and into everyone's lives. Endless possibilities existed. Government departments could exchange information and assemble profiles on all of us. They could make that information instantaneously available to our employers, to credit institutions, and to anyone else who was interested. Employers could exchange information about workers and their families. Mail order firms would have a ball. Data-banks could be assembled, and people would search out our tastes on everything from fruit to sex. The information would be sold to interested bodies, and computer searches would be instituted to find the natural markets for various products. Banks could instantaneously exchange information about customers and check every bank account. And Big Brother in the police and intelligence services would keep a very close eye on us.

In Europe and the United States proposals emerged to deal with this in the form of data protection legislation and data protection conventions. In the United States, freedom of access to information was a long-established principle, so the concern there was about preservation of privacy. In Europe, with a more secretive tradition, particularly in Britain and Ireland, it was clear that you couldn't really guarantee the privacy of data without allowing the citizens to know what data was kept on them. People had to be able to ensure that data about them was not transferred illegally, and that any data that might be transferred was accurate. The corollary was that you had to have the right to correct erroneous data. A Council of Europe convention was agreed in 1981 that was designed to protect privacy and guarantee access to records by individuals. It was gradually adopted by member-states, with Ireland displaying a bland indifference. Data protection was, after all, a function of the Department of Justice, and that department was never too keen on light being shed on any of its areas of interest.

This might have continued were it not for Charles Haughey's scheme to set up the International Financial Services Centre in Dublin. This was one of Mr Haughey's pet schemes, and his not inconsiderable self-esteem was invested in it. It emerged that no multinational banking organisation would come near Ireland if computer data-base privacy for banks' customers and a procedure for protecting the international transfer of data were not guaranteed. Something had to be done, and it had to be done quickly.

So they announced that they were ratifying the appropriate European convention, in the glorious tradition of the art of the possible. The then Minister for Justice, Gerry Collins, took up the cudgels on behalf of freedom and individual rights to information and unveiled the Data Protection Bill.

But not an inch more than was necessary was conceded. The Data Protection Act does give certain clear rights to individuals. People can, up to a point, seek details of information held on computer about them by the state or private agencies. People have the right, up to a point, to correct erroneous information, and they have the right, again up to a point, to insist that such information not be supplied to other people without their permission. But all the rights are qualified, particularly where the state is involved. As far as I can judge, every derogation possible under the convention was enthusiastically grasped by the Government—except one. This is contained in article 10 and allows governments 'to grant data subjects a wider measure of protection' than that provided by the convention. We apparently didn't need that.

On the other hand it was felt desirable that 'personal data that in the opinion of the Minister [for Justice] or the Minister for Defence are, or at any time were, kept for the purpose of safeguarding the security of the State' should not be covered by the act at all. Either minister can, without reference to anyone or appeal to anyone or without the subject ever knowing, exclude anything they want from the provisions of the act. The exclusion extends not just to existing data but to data that at any time was, in the opinion of either minister, kept 'for the purpose of safeguarding the security of the state.' Which brings us back to the 'security' merry-go-round from which we departed in chapter

5. Except that in this case the security of the state is retrospective!

Remember that the words quoted above are from an act of the Oireachtas, and each word is carefully considered by the parliamentary drafters before being inserted. So when the phrase 'in the opinion of' is used, this is done deliberately. The minister could have been required 'to be satisfied' instead of having an opinion. The Data Protection Commissioner could have been given a role. The courts could have been given at least an appeal function in the matter. Various other procedures could have been instituted. Instead we must rely on the *opinion* of the Minister for Justice or the Minister for Defence. Obviously it would be very difficult to disprove an 'opinion' in court. So our chances of seeing what's held about us under the great catch-all of 'national security' are more than remote.

Personal data kept by the state for purposes that the state deems to be related to national security may refer to earlier periods in a person's life, but the person is never to be allowed to know; the data may still be on record even if the person has long since moved away from what is called 'subversive' politics. The exclusion does not apply simply to data that is deemed necessary to protect the state: it applies if either of the ministers *thinks* it was ever held for that purpose. Even if the threat has receded, the data is to remain secret. And when you reflect on the breadth of definition given to the concept of 'the security of the state', as discussed in chapter 5, there is obviously an awful lot of data in the Government's possession but whose existence we will never be able to confirm.

Personal data held about members of the Garda Síochána and the Defence Forces is presumably covered by this exclusion, since it would obviously be the opinion of the ministers that keeping such data was necessary for the security of the state. But how much more is held? I wonder—perhaps mischievously—if the Department of Justice or indeed the Department of Defence has personal data on Michael D. Higgins. Will they tell him, or could they refuse? Is there personal data within the Department of Justice compiled 'to safeguard the security of the state' during Seán Doherty's period as Minister for Justice that we are never to know about?

I wrote to the Gardaí after the act became law and asked for access to any personal data they had on me. I was still a senator then, and assumed that the Gardaí, so careful in so many ways about the security of Leinster House and its occupants, must have information about the members of the Oireachtas in case of emergency, for example. The Gardaí assured me that they had no personal data on me. But of course if the 'personal data' they had on me was compiled to safeguard the security of the state they wouldn't have to admit to having it anyway.

That's not the only privilege the state claims for itself, though. It uses, as we've seen, every loophole available to it, and gives itself generous leeway by way of what appears to be a very flexible interpretation of ordinary language.

The convention provides that no exceptions are allowed other than in the interests of (*a*) protecting state security, public safety, the monetary interests of the state, or the suppression of criminal offences, and (*b*) protecting the 'data subject' or the rights and freedoms of others. We've seen how our Government has managed to stretch the concept of protecting state security to the extent of protecting data for ever, even if no risk to that security any longer exists. But when it comes to protecting the monetary interest of the state they give themselves even more leeway. The prohibition on disclosure of personal data is lifted if the disclosure is required, among other things, 'in assessing or collecting ... moneys owed or payable to ... a local authority or a health board.' So if you haven't paid your service charges or your hospital bill, the state can search every computerised record on you, and you have no legal redress under the Data Protection Act. Indeed they can even do that if they want to find out whether you *should* be paying something. They could even do it if you didn't pay a parking fine. And they don't have to tell you.

Indeed the priorities of the state are clear from the section of the act that deals with exemptions from its prohibition of disclosure of personal data. The first exemption relates to the security of the state and can be invoked either by a Garda chief superintendent or a colonel in the Defence Forces designated by the Minister for Defence. The second relates to the prevention of crime and extends to matters referred to earlier such as making you pay your service charges. The third, fourth and fifth relate to matters such as the need to protect property, the health and safety of an individual, court orders, and other legal and judicial matters.

Finally there is exception number 6, which says that data may be disclosed to the 'data subject'. Even though this little sub-section is no more than a tidying-up exercise, the priorities of the state are clear. It provides catch-all exemptions for itself, and then gets around to mentioning the rights of the individual in an act whose formal objective is the protection of that individual. The explanatory memorandum published when the bill was introduced is careful in its wording too. It says that a 'data controller' will still be subject to 'any such restrictions as may apply apart from those in the Bill.' They even say that the exemptions do 'not compel the disclosure of the personal data.' I'd love to tell that to a chief superintendent! There is a glorious fudge evident here that has little to do with the cause of privacy.

There are of course good things in the act. In the first place it gives some access to personal data held on computers. Not unexpectedly, it is also full of exceptions to that right. Some of these make sense (like the protection of data that would be legally privileged); but others reveal the same old attitudes. There is, inevitably, yet another 'security' exemption. This means you can be refused access to data held on yourself if it's kept 'for the purposes of protecting, detecting, or investigating offences.' This exclusion is extended to cover data held for reasons to do with tax, duty, or other financial matters (including, one presumes, service charges). The refusal is authorised 'in any case in which the application of the section would be likely to prejudice any of the matters aforesaid.' Further exceptions apply to the prisons, to information obtained from informers, and to personal data held to prevent malpractice by banks and similar institutions.

The legislation also acts as a severe restraint on many of those who hold large amounts of personal data. It at least attempts to stop them trading in personal data without the permission of the subject. It prevents banks from exchanging data about customers, or at least it's meant to. It should mean that Telecom

Éireann and the ESB could not exchange data about customers that might enable both to identify what are called 'consumer needs' more precisely. Other agencies would find this business extremely lucrative. Banks could deal with travel organisations, professional organisations with suppliers of goods and services. Computers have made all this extremely easy and potentially extremely lucrative, which explains Telecom Éireann's national life-style survey some years ago. They offered substantial prizes to participants in a competition who filled in a detailed life-style questionnaire. This was to be used to compile a data-base of information on customers that would be a significant resource for anyone in the consumer market. It would of course contain personal data that would be covered by the Data Protection Act, so they needed permission. They used a common device to get that. Down at the bottom of a long questionnaire, which was also a display brochure for the glittering prizes, we were told that the data given might be supplied to third parties and that if we didn't wish our data to be supplied we could indicate that. They gambled that most people would not read that far and would not tick the prohibition, and presumably they were right.

An Post has a similar scheme in operation. It's called 'Targetpoint', and is described in publicity as a data-base on life-style. The information was assembled from a similar questionnaire, and is available for use at a fee. We are fortunate, however, that they are prevented from doing more, as the information would be extremely valuable.

They have to behave because of the vigilance of the Data Protection Commissioner, who is appointed under the act. The first commissioner was vigilant and determined and set the tone for the future. Indeed his annual report for 1991 outlines clearly the level of concern he had about a number of issues. He reprimanded many of those in the credit and credit reference business for a lack of transparency and less than acceptable 'standards of accuracy and relevance.' But his most substantial criticisms were of the state. He detailed what was obviously a momentous struggle with the Department of Social Welfare. They were seeking to compel third-level colleges to supply the name and address of registered students to them. The commissioner saw this as a breach of the right to privacy and succeeded in preventing the department from obtaining any more data from the colleges than what they clearly required for the purposes of the act. It is obvious from the tone of the report that the commissioner felt the department would have had a wonderful time trawling through students' personal data if he hadn't intervened. But he reserved his strongest words for a proposal to introduce a 'universal identity number'. He says: 'This proposal was made with scant reference to the Data Protection Act, and with little evidence to show that its implications had been studied or researched.' It was never proceeded with, and we can thank the Data Protection Commissioner for that, and for his subsequent success in toning down the Department of Education's proposal to give all second-level students a universal number.

Clearly the area of electronic data is to some extent regulated, and the act works well where it hasn't been deliberately emasculated by the state. Unfortunately it has one overwhelming defect: it applies only to computerised data. Neither the restrictions on disclosure nor the right to access to data, nor the right to correct inaccurate material, applies to manually compiled and stored material, that is, to records that are kept on paper or on microfilm. Masses of material are kept in that fashion, much of it, one presumes, deliberately. The network of parish priests who share information on potential national teachers would be well advised, and would not keep such information on computer: a print-out of a legal computer data-base with a few additional handwritten notes would do the job perfectly.

Parish priests are well advised on such matters. So are bank managers and members of the Gardaí and army. Employers too would have access to such advice; and many third-level colleges ensure that details of student assessments and other matters are kept in manual files. It is not difficult to envisage memorandums that might circulate in large institutions advising people how to meet both the requirements of the Data Protection Act and the organisation's desire to hold on to sensitive information, without consulting the subject of the information. Given the Data Protection Commissioner's strictures on the operations of financial and credit institutions where they are covered by the Data Protection Act, one must conclude that privacy and accuracy would be even less regarded by them in their manual records.

In every area of the country there is a suspicion that employers' groups have available to them black-lists of workers whom they are advised not to recruit. The reasons might sometimes be convincing: no-one wants to hire someone who has a record of unnecessary absenteeism, or anti-social behaviour. But neither do employers, particularly those who have non-unionised work forces, want to hire people who might have a record of trade union activism. But convincing or not, information such as that, if stored electronically, is covered by the Data Protection Act and cannot be supplied to interested third parties other than in the situations prescribed by the act. Furthermore, it would probably have to be made available to the person concerned for correction. Paper records are clearly preferable, and obviously people are aware of this.

There was clear evidence of the attitude of public authorities to such records when Dublin City Council was involved in attempts to move on travellers and tried to introduce social workers' files as evidence in the case. This was a clear example of data that had been collected for one purpose being used for something entirely different. Such a use of electronically stored data would be prohibited under the Data Protection Act; these files, however, were in manual form, and no clear legal—as distinct from ethical—prohibition existed. Fortunately the staff involved resisted, and the management desisted.

Nevertheless it does leave one wondering what happens when state bodies are making judgments about people. What procedures are there to ensure that at a case conference involving, say, medical social work and housing staff the information supplied is accurate, up to date, and only supplied to an extent necessitated by the needs of the person being discussed? It would be nice to believe that the spirit of the Data Protection Act would be applied, since that is supposed to represent the view of society about the right to privacy. Unfortunately, given the attitude of public bodies to their obligations under the act, it's easy to believe that the administrative convenience of data exchange will soon dissipate any such spirit!

That is why the recent proposals of the EU to produce a Directive on Data Protection are to be welcomed, if only because it is proposed that the directive should cover all data, however stored. Unfortunately the directive will only cover the areas of competence of the EU and will presumably not involve security or related matters, which, we are assured, are still matters for the national government.

10 FROM THE CRADLE TO THE GRAVE

● ●

The Data Protection Act is obviously flawed, but a brief look at the number of agencies that retain large amounts of data about us on computer will remind us how important it is, and how much more needs to be done. As we look through the range of organisations and the data they hold on us it's difficult to avoid repetition of the old cliché about information and power.

The following agencies, among others, keep large amounts of data on us:

Department of Social Welfare
Department of Education
Department of Justice
Department of Foreign Affairs
Revenue Commissioners
ESB
Telecom Éireann
An Post
Local authorities
Health boards

As well as these there is the central car registration computer in Shannon, which can be accessed by the Gardaí and local authorities directly.

The ESB will have records going back over all the occasions when we opened an account with them. They will also have records from any occasion when we bought an appliance from them on credit. That record will contain details of their adjudication on our creditworthiness, and will be used by them for future credit purchases.

The Department of Social Welfare has records on us going back to birth, if our mothers claimed children's allowances—and unless you're pushing a hundred that's most likely to be the case! In those records they have details of our parentage, of our parents' names, etc. As we progress through life they will assign us a PRSI number, and under that number they will have records of all the places we worked and all the benefits we may have claimed. This will include periods of unemployment, periods of disability, and indeed periods of low income when we might have claimed family income supplement. They will also know if we in turn claim child benefit for our children, and the rigmarole will start again. And of course if you marry, all that information is added to the data-base. Given the amount of information they have on us, it is both understandable and welcome that the Data Protection Commissioner took such a dim view of the magnetic card proposal referred to earlier. If it had got going as they had wished we would have ended up having many of our personal details stored on a machine-readable card. The card would have had an irresistible appeal to gardaí, even at traffic checks. It would have simplified the job of health boards enormously, and would also greatly help the Department of Education. They could have argued plausibly that the information available to Social Welfare would help them to identify schools with a high proportion of socially deprived children. But then plausible reasons for invasion of privacy are two a penny.

The electronic mountain grows on, however. The Revenue Commissioners also assemble vast amounts of information on us, and, as we saw earlier, our rights of access to that data may well be quite restricted. They too have our PRSI number, and under that have better records of our income and other history than we often have ourselves. They know exactly where we worked, and how much we earned. They know how much interest we are paying on our mortgage (indeed they have direct access to building society computers to find that out), and they knew until recently how much life insurance we had. As well as that they are up to date with our marital status; they know when we separate, and they will usually know when an unmarried couple set up house together.

Health boards too are entitled to know a lot about us. They must find out in order to assess our eligibility for hospital services and for medical cards. And of course since there is no such thing as a universal means test, the health boards will seek information from us that perhaps the Department of Social Welfare or the Revenue Commissioners didn't want. And they may all be entitled to demand access to each other's computerised records if we're overdue with a payment for a hospital charge or a local authority charge. Pursuit of those charges might well allow local authorities to dig into the other computers too.

The Department of Foreign Affairs too must have considerable data stored about us, or at least about those of us who have or ever had a passport. A considerable amount of detail is supplied on passport application forms, and even more on the parental consent form. Yet again all that data can be accessed by the public authorities for any of the broad exemption categories, even the ones to do with paying your service charges!

But at least in those areas the Data Protection Act applies. In the case of the Departments of Defence and Justice we know nothing. They may well have accessed all our personal files from time to time and copied large amounts of the information onto their own computers. They may well have erroneous records about us. They may routinely update their files on all of us. We won't know, because the act doesn't apply to them if their ministers say so, and their ministers don't have to tell us if they say so: that's a secret too! What is not secret is their insatiable nosiness. If they were prepared to go to considerable lengths to find out about CND and the Irish Housewives' Association long before computer data interchange became so easy, one can only imagine what their appetite for information must be now.

At least, however, public authorities don't *sell* the information they have on us. They may misuse the information from time to time, but they don't show any inclination to pass it on at a profit to others. 'Semi-state' bodies, while obviously operating within the letter of the law, are not so sensitive. An Post, as we saw earlier, offers a service called 'Targetpoint', subtitled 'Irish Consumer and Household Information'. They offer to supply labels, magnetic tape or disks of information on consumers and households. They can select on the basis of location, sex, socio-economic category, property ownership, age, number of children, or special interests. They boast of their achievement in 'the application of the very latest census of population statistics' to a postal questionnaire to give 'a profile of over 2.5 million adults'. And, as they say themselves, 'it doesn't end there'. They say they 'will be targeting at least 50,000 Irish households every month' to keep their information accurate. And they will sell this information to you. They will give you labels addressed to people with the range of interests, income etc. you are interested in, at a price of £80 per thousand upwards.

So much for data protection, you might say. But none of this is illegal. That is because, in their own quaint language, 'all prospects have bypassed a negative option to receive Direct Mail offers,' which actually means they have signed away their rights under the Data Protection Act. An Post add helpfully that 'all individuals are mail responsive and have returned a questionnaire to us by post.' So we should all tick those little boxes at the bottom of questionnaires!

But a more serious question arises. An Post have this obviously comprehensive data-base detailing our every preference and prejudice. They are clearly covered by the Data Protection Act in the way they supply that information. But what about the other exemptions under the act? Can local authorities looking for details about us in connection with non-payment of service charges, or health boards in connection with medical bills, compulsorily access data-bases such as 'Targetpoint'? It appears that the act doesn't impose an obligation on 'data controllers' to supply the information. All that the exemptions are alleged to mean is that those in charge of personal data are freed from their obligation to refuse disclosure. The obvious question then is, why have the exemptions at all? The answer I think was provided by the explanatory memorandum. This pointed out that 'data controllers' were still subject to 'any such restrictions as may apply' apart from those in the act. It didn't say that 'data controllers' without protection under the act are also subject to whatever obligations they may have under other legislation.

The mention of census data raises a question. The Data Protection Act obviously covers information obtained from the census. Can the Gardaí access the data-bases of the Central Statistics Office—bearing in mind their general powers, the exemption we've already mentioned, and their well-documented nosiness? We know that the CSO staff are committed to absolute confidentiality and are utterly trustworthy in that regard. But can they be sure that they always know what's being done? The act says nothing about whether records must be kept by anyone who supplies or obtains data under the various exemptions in the act. It does not even require records to be kept. And of course the data might not even be obtained by means of the CSO at all: it is quite conceivable that elements of the Gardaí or army already possess the necessary access to enable them to 'hack' into any computer in the country. They are, after all, not prohibited under the act from seeking the information, and they might need it urgently. And of course if the minister is of the opinion that they need it then we won't find out if they ever get it! And because of the blanket exemption we can't even ensure that such data is only obtained legally.

This still leaves us more or less within the realms of the law. We may not approve of certain activities of the Gardaí or army, but given the powers they have under various bits of legislation, hardly anything they might do in the information field could ever be thought prima facie to be illegal.

What is illegal is the practice of 'hacking' in to computer data-bases either for profit or for fun. Indeed the illegal use of computers is now a serious source of loss and fraud. Some people estimate that millions of pounds disappear in Ireland through computer fraud. Institutions and computer suppliers are not very forthcoming on the matter, and financial institutions are adamant that their own computers are completely secure. In particular they insist that it is impossible for their ATMs (cash-dispensing machines) to make mistakes. So far the ombudsman for the credit institutions supports their contention, but there is a little bit of the 'finger in the dike' about their assurances. Anything more than a superficial knowledge of the computer business and its associated literature will add to this impression.

It is apparent from that literature that increased security is a matter of great concern to computer users and a significant source of business for suppliers of both software and hardware. It's a reasonable inference that that concern is not imaginary. It has been evident for years, and shows no sign of lessening, so we can presume that it is the product of experience. There are also obviously good commercial reasons why breaches of computer security would not be widely publicised. I do know that some years ago a student in a Dublin university quite by accident generated a print-out of the account details of many of the customers of one of the big banks. Newspaper reports too seem to confirm the view that computer security is still far from perfected. The *Evening Herald* of 24 January 1994 reported that a number of 'investigation' agencies were prepared, for relatively small sums of money, to provide them with any unlisted telephone number they wished, and one did just that! Telecom Éireann and various experts asserted that it was more likely a breach of security by an employee than a breach of their computer security. That explanation seems credible when the information is held by one particular organisation; it falls down a bit when it turns out that the same 'investigation' agencies asserted that they could supply details of anyone's personal bank account. The availability of this information requires access to the data-bases of each of the individual banks. It is hard to believe that there is an efficient, well-hidden and unknown 'mole' working for every one of the banks that have branches in Dublin. So, however much the experts may deny it, the most likely explanation remains that the information is obtained by 'hacking' into the appropriate computer. Indeed, given the relatively low price demanded for the information (less than fifty pounds), it would all appear to have been relatively routine.

It is obvious from this and the previous chapter that the Data Protection Act is porous in the extreme. Exceptions that, in the Council of Europe convention, were clearly designed to protect a state from fundamental threats to its institutions have been distorted to provide cover for ministerial discomfort. A clause that is clearly meant to enable the state to defend its currency and deal with large-scale tax evasion is used to minimise restrictions on the access powers of every local authority and health board in pursuit of the most trivial sums of money.

To cap it all, Big Brother, in the guise of the Ministers for Justice and Defence, is still watching, or may be watching, or was watching, or whatever is justified in the opinion of the minister of the time. Because the act, popularly thought to be designed to protect us from Big Brother, in effect exempts Big Brother from all legal restraint.

Part 3
Reclaiming Our Own

11

WORKING FOR US — FOR A CHANGE

● ●

Though Ireland is a haven of institutionalised secrecy, there are many ways of discovering a lot of what our betters would prefer we didn't know. We'll look first at the public sector, move on to the public-private interface, and finish with the private sector, though it's difficult to actually identify a genuinely private sector in Ireland. Indeed, as we've seen, one of the peculiarities of Ireland is that the public sector has gone to such extraordinary lengths to protect the privacy of private business, however small.

The Government has sought, and obtained, derogations from EU disclosure regulations because of the sensitivity of what they insist on calling small Irish industry. What we are more often than not protecting are the Irish subsidiaries of multinationals, whose managements can often succeed in hiding a good deal of their international business under the guise of fragile 'Irish' small business. And of course while we do that we happily advertise the commercial secrets, the competitive advantages and the market power of many of our biggest companies, that is, those in the state sector. Nevertheless it is hard not to conclude that the private sector benefits from the state's obsessive fretting about disclosure.

But let us return for the time being to the public sector. During my political career I took to offering unsolicited advice to pressure groups on how to be effective. My advice was always that there were at least three if not ten prerequisites for successful lobbying. The first was stamina, the second was more stamina, and the third was more stamina again, and if there was a fourth and a fifth and on up to a tenth I would still say it. So rule 1: *Stamina!*

Other things, such as knowledge, persistence, contacts, presentation, publicity, and so on, are of course important. But for all those to work the fundamental resource is limitless stamina. It is difficult to get information out of the public sector. At the high-powered level of senior civil servants and the Government, this may well be because of policy factors. On occasions on Oireachtas committees I have been driven close to screaming and yet grudgingly impressed by the sheer ingenuity of civil servants who have been given the job of not telling a committee what the minister didn't want the committee to know. I have often believed that the greatest asset senior civil servants have is the extent to which opinion-formers, media people and other 'luminaries' underestimate them. Anyone who has had the opportunity of reading a ministerial brief on a difficult issue comes away with a different view! Who else could possibly come near their ability to think of every option? Mind you, having a monopoly on the flow of information helps a lot!

But that's at a formal level. It is not universal. Indeed the earlier obstacles to access to information are mostly inertia rather than policy. So the next rule of information-seeking is: *Find out who might have it, and ask.*

This sounds trivial; but I could cite hundreds of cases where it wasn't done. Civil servants can be remarkably forthcoming if you ask, with some precision, for information. On one occasion I succeeded in embarrassing Pádraig Flynn thanks to civil servants in his department. The minister was introducing a new Water Pollution Bill in the Seanad and was, as only that minister could be, effusive in praise of himself for his diligence. I discovered that a previous water pollution bill made provision for a good deal of planning and policy-making that would not have required much money. It would, though, have required considerable ministerial interest. I thought I'd like to know how much had been done. There were no public records I could find; so I rang the department and asked for the information. I was promptly supplied with everything I wanted to know, and a bit more besides. I used the information a day later, at least temporarily, to slow down P. Flynn's gallop!

Departments are usually awash with information, and notwithstanding the theory, not all, indeed not many, decisions are taken in the immortal 'I am directed by the minister' fashion. You depend on your judgment, and Government departments depend on their own staff too.

This is all only true of course if you are asking for precise and more or less factual information. And there is no point ringing the Department of Finance and asking for your local TD's expenses record. Likewise there is no point in ringing the Department of Justice, full stop.

This work can be a lot easier if you get your hands on two books. The first of these is the *IPA Yearbook and Diary*, published annually by the Institute of Public Administration. It's expensive, though it's also available in libraries. In it you'll find the names of most senior civil servants and many less senior ones as well. You'll find the names of the staff of the minister's office, and may get clues about who might be best informed on the matter you're interested in. The phone gets you through, and you can't be put off in the way a letter can. And of course once you have the name and an admission of some responsibility you've made progress. After that it's down to rule 1, stamina, again.

There is a second, less well-known source of information. This is *Eolaire an Stáit*, the state directory, available from the Government bookshop, Molesworth Street, Dublin. This contains the name, function, location and in many cases salary of virtually the entire civil service. It gives some idea of who is responsible for what, and will point you in the right direction.

Many departments publish annual reports. The Department of Social Welfare, for instance, publishes an annual report that, while glossy and propaganda-oriented, can often be a significant source of information. Similarly the annual reports of the Revenue Commissioners are well worth reading. There you'll discover that there are only five thousand self-employed people with incomes greater than £25,000 a year. Information like that can seriously damage your stamina!

If you are looking for large amounts of information or for comparative statistics, then you may need more than a phone call and a chat: you may need a bit of influence. Here is where the much-maligned multi-seat constituency can come to your assistance. TDs and senators are not in a position to take you for granted. Even if their party has one or two or three safe seats in your constituency, each TD is transfixed by the prospect of losing his or her seat. (Given my own recent experience, they are probably right!) The preoccupation is not so much with the rival party as with rivals from their own party. Indeed intra-party rivalry nowadays is a good deal more bitter (and often verging on the violent) than inter-party rivalry. Use that to your advantage.

There are, however, a number of different kinds of politicians to contact when seeking information. If you are looking for information that you think important but that won't result in trouble for the Government, then approach your local Government TDs or senators. Explain in writing what you want and ask them to find out. In most cases they will be happy to oblige. Because they have a party colleague in the Government they are in a position to persuade a reluctant official to be helpful. It will help if you outline your own unsuccessful efforts in this regard.

It is probably wiser to deal with only one member of a party at a time. If they all know you're working on them they'll suspect that they'll get little enough credit for anything they do. And it's perfectly reasonable for them to be hoping for some credit. It's the nature of the business, and not in the least corrupt or unsavoury. My experience is that few enough people contact politicians unless they have a personal grievance they want sorted out.

Politicians have access to ministers, Government departments and civil servants with an ease that only the super-rich or super-powerful outside politics can match. What you should be concerned about is what they do with that access. Information of a global nature is not something they seek with any regularity, but they can get it. You may have to gently but persistently remind them that you want something, though, because of its non-routine nature. Because ordinary politicians have far more work to do than they are given credit for, less persistent demands will go to the bottom of the pile.

If you want information that might not be helpful to the Government, then your best bet is obviously an opposition TD. You won't necessarily find them immediately more sympathetic, so a little sugar on the pill will help. Explain what you want the information for and how perhaps they could use it themselves. It's particularly useful if you give them an issue that might generate a bit of favourable publicity locally.

Remember, though, that even if your local TDs fail you it's worth pursuing the matter further. The six university senators, for instance, have national constituencies and will often be happy to look for information that an average TD might find uninteresting or embarrassing. Try to find out too about the interests or specialisations of politicians from around the country. Some may have an interest in foreign affairs, others in environmental matters, and so on. If they have, then they may find that you can be as helpful to them as they are to you.

Make sure too to find out who precisely in opposition parties has which area of responsibility. Front-benchers from the bigger opposition parties have privileges that could be very useful in extracting information or at the very least in highlighting a refusal to disclose it.

So far we've only looked at the informal ways in which the political system can be used to get information. There are other very useful formal methods.

To the outsider the Dáil and Seanad seem to alternate between juvenile name-calling and formalised and mind-destroying boredom. And they do give rise to a lot of both; but they are also a good deal more powerful than most people, including journalists who report on them, realise. This is because politics is not just about who has a majority in the Dáil, in which numbers determine absolute power and the absence thereof the opposite. It would be so if ministers and politicians were ruthless, thick-skinned, insensitive brutes indifferent to the ordinary ups and downs of life. In reality they are (though their behaviour would try to contradict it) extraordinarily sensitive to criticism. Every word of critical comment is taken seriously and pondered over. Don't ever believe the politicians who tell you they never read the paper or watch television. They're having you on. It's because they realise how vulnerable they are that they pretend it doesn't affect them. And of course when you think about it it's that sensitivity to other people's opinions and a deep-seated need for approval that drives on all of us who have contested elections. I've come to the conclusion that in fact the temperament that drives people into politics is probably the temperament that is least suited to the practice of the modern, ruthless, intensely competitive form of politics!

Nevertheless it's that almost universal vulnerability that makes the two houses of the Oireachtas so much more than simple ritual debating chambers with predictable outcomes and absolute power. And that's why they can be so useful in extracting information. Ministers like to say yes, whatever the advice they receive! If they say no they prefer to do it obliquely, at the end of a treatise on all the good things they have done. But the way the Oireachtas works can reduce dramatically the number of ways they have of avoiding that responsibility.

The simplest method of all is the written question. Every member of the Dáil can ask an unlimited number of these, and will get an answer three days after the question is submitted. If you, therefore, have a good idea of the information you desire and are sure which minister is responsible, a written Dáil question could at least save you a lot of work and at best extract information that has not previously been published. But written questions often get unsatisfactory replies. One TD friend of mine once asked a question for me in an effort to find out what proportion of a proposed public service pay rise would return to the Government as taxes and levies. The reply, in writing, from Bertie Ahern was that it was impossible to estimate that figure. Which was a bit hard to take, given that the minister was responsible for paying all the salaries and also, through the Revenue Commissioners, for collecting all the taxes. But in the midst of negotiations about public service pay an estimate of the kind looked for would have been powerful information for the trade unions.

But if a written question doesn't succeed, an oral question is worth trying. In the lottery that is used to select oral questions, persistence, as always, can pay. Once a question is down for oral answer the minister will be more vigilant and perhaps more forthcoming. A well-briefed opposition questioner can often persuade a minister to promise further information.

And it need not end there. The top-ranking questions are 'priority' questions. These can only be asked by the large opposition parties. They are usually anxious to make as big an impact as possible and will therefore be quite receptive to suggestions for questions that might extract information a Government would prefer not to be noticed. So it's worth knowing who the appropriate spokespersons are and finding out a little about their own special interests.

Information can often be obtained too during debates on proposed legislation. It's worth while, therefore, keeping an eye on the Dáil order paper (and the Seanad's as well) to see what business is being discussed and when. Get in early with your information and questions. A front-bencher will be ecstatic if you can leave him or her with five or six awkward questions to ask a minister when the legislation is first debated. It was in this fashion that I discovered that, notwithstanding the perpetual fuss about welfare 'abuse' and the regular hysterical claims, not a single doctor had ever been reported to the Medical Council by the Department of Social Welfare for fraudulent certification.

Ministers are usually prepared to go a long way to meet requests for information that relates to a particular bill. This is both, as I've said earlier, because of their nature and because of the process through which legislation is dealt with by the Oireachtas. After the set-piece speeches of the second stage comes the committee stage, during which the legislation will (usually!) be gone through line by line. This stage is tedious, it bores journalists to death, but it is the period in the Oireachtas when a minister is most accessible, least protected, and in other words most easily got at. It can be tougher on a minister than any media interview, because in many instances there will be in effect no time limit. No minister will therefore want to add further to his or her troubles by refusing information: he or she knows that the opposition will only come back even more strongly at the committee stage. And because of the relatively informal procedures involved, the committee will be able to pursue the matter endlessly and mercilessly. Common sense alone would dictate that a minister set as few traps for himself or herself as possible. The fact that the minister will win a vote if one is called is no consolation if he or she is being publicly put through a wringer by a well-informed opposition. I had a run-in with a badly briefed junior minister once on the topic of licences to sell liquor in restaurants. That was years ago, and he is still talking about it.

The need for limitless stamina is surely obvious by now. None of what I've advocated is effortless, but neither would it be plain sailing to plough through mountains of Government documents released under a Freedom of Information Act. It is also clear that you need to know a bit about the information you're looking for. You need to know what department it's in. You need to be able to explain to your chosen politician why you need it, in language that will make sense to him or her, and you need to know under what proposed legislation you hope to extract the desired knowledge. Nevertheless it can work. I've done it myself for my own purposes and I've also done it for others who required particular information. And most of the preliminary work I've described here would be necessary even if we were to have the benefit of a Freedom of Information Act on the scale of the American version.

Of course the limitations of this approach are fairly obvious. First of all there are no guarantees involved. Ministers can invoke custom and practice as well as the law to refuse information. They are also entitled to refuse to answer a question if they feel that the amount of work involved would be excessive. And, as in my enquiry about taxes, they can sometimes just refuse!

As well as that we are only dealing with areas of the state that are directly under the control of central government. Local authorities, health boards and VECs are only accessible to the extent that their information is available to Government departments. But even here, since we are such an extraordinarily centralised country, central government has its finger in virtually every local pie. (We'll come back later to local bodies.)

The other main area of difficulty is the 'semi-state' sector. There is no ministerial responsibility here, and questions in the Dáil will be disallowed. In addition, the simple expedient of buying a single share, very useful in the private sector, isn't available either. So we'll have to return to them too.

The greatest inhibition to more widespread use of the procedures we've looked at, however, is the expected failure of the chosen politician to produce the goods. This expectation usually arises from hearsay rather than experience. People may try once; they get the usual assurance and then they wait. Over and over again I am told by people that they've tried all the politicians and heard nothing. So they give up. Almost invariably this is because of the suspicion that if you keep after them they'll get annoyed and abandon you. After all, that's how the rest of humanity would respond. It's difficult to overstate the extent to which people are wrong about this. They seem to see politicians as fickle donors of favours, liable to be put off by the first sight of pressure, complaint, or harassment. They are used to grim-faced politicians in suitably impressive surroundings endlessly repeating the mantra of power: 'We will not yield to pressure.' And the system expects this repetition, indeed it needs it to survive.

But endless repetition doesn't make something true. The truth is that politicians always give in to pressure. Pressure is the index of priority that politicians (and I include my own career in this) respond to with the greatest sensitivity and intensity. They prefer rational argument, but they listen to pressure. Pressures from different sources sometimes compete, but when you see a political leader publicly identify a source of pressure and repeat again, 'We won't give in to that,' it probably means that they're giving in to another, perhaps less visible but more forceful pressure.

So if it's information you're after, you have to persuade your selected political ally that you are informed, persistent, permanent, and determined. You must, if necessary, become a nuisance. Remember always that he or she cannot take the risk of telling you to get lost. They don't know whether others are being more helpful. They don't know who you voted for the last time—and they don't know which of their party rivals may be burrowing away on your behalf.

There is of course no need to be rude or offensive, nor to pursue someone to their home. Leinster House is a remarkably open place in terms of telephone access. There are few enough filters, and a phone call to a politician's office is as likely to be answered by the politician as by his or her secretary or assistant. And of course if the tone of voice suggests that patience is wearing thin stay polite, but stay! At this stage you're winning. It might even be worth while suggesting alternative courses of action. It will give a clear impression that you are both persistent and informed. A suggestion of a Dáil question or an approach to a minister or front-bencher might well be welcomed by a harassed back-bencher.

Don't forget, though, that this is only one of a number of routes to information. Remember too that legislation has to go through both houses of the Oireachtas. A thorough reading of the debate in one house can give a lot of clues for fruitful approaches to prospective contributors in the other house.

This, however, doesn't get us any closer to finding out about the semi-state sector. Indeed some would say that that's one of the reasons why more and more bodies are being given separate legal status. It takes the day-to-day heat off ministers, and it enables many bodies to cloak themselves in the particular brand of secrecy that is the hallmark of Irish business.

But they're not impervious either. They do publish annual reports, and while usually these are essentially PR exercises, they contain useful information. The IDA's annual report contains lots of information about who gets grants and who promised jobs. RTE doesn't give much away, but their budget analysis can be useful and informative.

The best way to dig in a semi-state body, however, is through the Oireachtas Committee on State-Sponsored Bodies. I believe this is one of the most powerful committees, and there are always some good, able back-benchers on it. If you contact Leinster House the staff of the committee will let you have the committee's planned programme of business. You will then have a time scale within which to prepare questions and contact members of the committee. Don't be shy! The members will be glad to get their hands on useful angles to pursue. Indeed they are usually in a position to get preliminary answers to questions before the formal meeting of the committee. And if you have been in 'dialogue' with a particular politician, announce that you'd like to attend the public hearings. It will help the concentration immensely!

There is one obvious consequence of all this. That is that the Dáil and Seanad records often contain lots of useful information. A journalist-politician once told me that he was convinced that there is probably a good story in Dáil questions every day if only someone would bother to look. So look!

12 FINDING OUT ABOUT THE COMMUNITY

● ●

W hile looking for local information may seem like a
sophisticated version of the Valley of the Squinting
Windows, it is in reality no more than a confirmation
of Tip O'Neill's immortal insistence on the importance of local
politics. And at local level there is not much that is not political.

At the level of the community with which people identify,
little happens that doesn't involve a fairly delicate balancing of
interests and personnel. When a parish council is being
assembled, the careful parish priest will ensure that the various
factions within the parish are balanced. Episcopal nominations to
school boards of management will reflect an attempt to balance
the various forces within the parish, though of course the parish
priest will usually assert that the appointments are made by the
bishop, leaving the clear implication that there was no local
influence. Similar efforts will go into the structure of most other
voluntary organisations. And those who have been dominant in
voluntary organisations, whatever their purpose, are usually more
than capable of deflecting any attempts to change their pet
organisation. This will be confirmed by many a young idealist
who tried to change their local St Vincent de Paul conference or
GAA club. Indeed when you watch the manoeuvrings in and
around all these bodies you can't but wonder at the way so many
get away with the assertion that they want to keep 'above
politics'. What they really mean is that they recognise the politics

of it all but want to keep it firmly under their control. The kind of politics such local operators are 'above' is usually the kind they can't control!

That the 'real' politics is not much different will be confirmed by the hundreds of young hopefuls who over the years have tried to change local political structures. The bloodletting that was part and parcel of Garret FitzGerald's reorganisation of Fine Gael demonstrated that clearly. The Labour Party will confirm that one constituency was dominated for years by a single man. It was often said that the membership registered for that particular constituency was well in excess of the total vote the party used to get there at general elections! Retirement was the decisive factor ultimately: when he retired, they reorganised.

Even now it is surprising what you can find out locally if you are in earnest. In the case of state agencies the best place to begin is with the law. Statutory agencies after all are not allowed to operate in complete secrecy, though many would prefer to do so. The law imposes considerable duties on them. Local authorities do publish accounts and must keep records. If you can't get them, ask a sympathetic local representative to find out why not. Ask him or her in particular to find out the statutory authority under which information is being withheld. If the reply is 'custom and practice' or that it's 'contrary to policy', then ask the councillor in question to put down a motion seeking to change the rules. Ask him or her to make it known that they're doing it.

It's probably best to find an independent councillor to do this, since they will tend to be less than enamoured with the club atmosphere that usually prevails. This is because, very often, independents are excluded from the committees and officerships of local authorities. They are therefore more likely to be prepared to disturb the peace. They may not succeed in getting the rule changed immediately, but they will begin a process that a sustained local campaign will often complete. You could follow this up by visiting local authority offices and asking to inspect draft reports, estimates, accounts, and plans. Ask for the number on the housing list, for the housing allocation procedure adopted, and for a copy of the council's standing orders. Read these carefully and you may well be able to advise your sympathetic councillor on how to ambush the routine procedures. He or she will get some publicity, and you will have advanced the cause of accountability. A good idea would be to ask for the criteria the council adopts in deciding which matters should be discussed in private.

Make sure to get the councillor to ask for details of travelling and other expenses paid to members. The best procedure here would be to find a member who lives close to where meetings are held and who is also outside the magic circle who have shared out the committees, mayoralty or chairmanship and, usually, junkets between them. He or she will have no compunction about asking, because the council can't take away privileges he or she hasn't got, and the councillor will get lots of publicity.

You could help by becoming a regular attender at meetings yourself and noting the pattern of attendance of members. Count the number who are there to record attendance at the beginning of meetings, and watch the drop-off as the day or evening goes on. Do it a few times and see if you can observe a pattern. Then contact the local media. Let them know what you have found out, and ask them to seek further information. If the information is not forthcoming do a reasonable assessment yourself of the maximum a councillor can make out of allowances and expenses, and publicise that, without of course mentioning names. Just be sure that you are estimating maximum values. This will provoke an outcry of denial. Invite them then to publicise the true figures. You will nevertheless have established the precedent. The figures will be published.

Continue the tactics wherever you find secrecy that is not explicitly demanded by statute. If they say it's secret, ask for the rules, and ask which rule they used. Usually they make it up as they go along and have a remarkable tendency to confuse the public interest with their own convenience. A report in the *Evening Herald* early in January 1994 illustrated this well. The paper had reported unflatteringly on the attendance record of members of Dublin City Council. The members retaliated by making their attendance records secret! Quite probably they can't do that, but it would take a court action to sort it out. The procedure I suggested earlier, of watching them at the beginning of the meeting and as the numbers drop—a mild form of direct action—would achieve the same result. Even if you can't do it yourself a fiver to a person with time on their hands would give you as much return as the expense of a High Court challenge!

You still haven't exhausted your weaponry. Remember that there's lots of information local authorities may have that they are obliged to give to you. That includes environmental data. This of course extends far beyond large industries and their waste streams. Ask them when was the last time the exhaust of local authority vehicles was analysed; ask them how many prosecutions for litter offences there have been; ask them the condition of effluent from the local sewage treatment plant, or the local butchers or the local bakery. They are supposed to know. Push them hard enough and they'll find out, and when they find out they'll have to tell you.

Remember that many of the powers and responsibilities of local authorities are 'reserved' functions: this means that the ultimate responsibility rests with the senior executive of the authority, the county or city manager or town clerk. The county manager system was introduced as a response to apparently well-grounded allegations of corruption in local authorities. Allegations were made that local authority housing was obtained in this way, for instance, and that jobs were allocated according to party political favouritism. The managerial system was meant to introduce a standard of professionalism that would eliminate the corruption, and it has succeeded reasonably well. Where modern local authorities make suspect decisions nowadays it is the members who usually make them against the advice of the officials; rezoning and 'section 4' decisions are obvious examples of this.

But if you want information about reserved functions you must deal with officialdom. And officialdom, while not corrupt, is not, at local level at least, very enthusiastic about letting us know what is going on. An obvious example would be in the area of housing allocation. The decisions are made by the housing officer according to fairly thorough criteria, but the housing officer is rarely directly accessible to applicants or to community groups. Social workers, sworn to secrecy, are usually the interface. This system avoids the corruption that goes with unaccountable influence, but it leaves intact the aberrations that can spring from unaccountable power. Public representatives can deal with the housing officer, but they are not likely to trouble him or her too severely, since they will always be dependent on him or her for information, and indeed for decisions.

Matters to do with travellers are also subject to a good deal of unaccountable bureaucracy. This happens even though elected representatives are required to take the final decision about locations for halting sites. It is not clear that the subsequent running of such sites is a matter of concern to the elected representatives. I suspect that such organisational detail is not a matter for councillors; the consequence is that centres of power develop that are not under democratic control. Where the person in charge is well disposed, this usually means good sites, good services, and progress. When the person in charge is not, then we have the worst possible manifestation of power without accountability. I visited one large official halting site and saw conditions worse than I saw in a Palestinian refugee camp in Gaza. Electricity had been cut off, and water was restricted to one tap. There were no road surfaces, and sanitation was primitive. A negative attitude on the part of the person in charge can create impossible obstacles for the travellers, care workers, and elected representatives. Travellers hope they can move on, carers can be intimidated, and elected representatives often remain silent.

How to deal with such situations? It seems to me that there is a clear common approach to be taken, irrespective of the issue. It could be about refuse collection in your area or the local dump or traffic or water quality or anything. We will assume it is about a travellers' halting site and that you want conditions improved, because this is a particularly difficult one where you could not expect much local support. The first thing to do obviously is to assemble independent information, that is, information that is not dependent on people who would be vulnerable or feel vulnerable to any sort of retribution. Talk to the local clergy, and to the teachers who have the care of children from the place. Walk around the place yourself, and take a few photographs.

Confirm with residents of the site that conditions are as you suspect.

Then assure yourself that the individual local authority officer identified is really the person responsible. This is extremely important, because the accountable person may not be the person whose name appears at the bottom of correspondence. I discovered this through an encounter with Dublin City Council one time that left me wondering even more about what is done in our names. I received a copy of a letter concerning access by guide dogs to a particular building. The letter from the official was an astonishing amalgam of prejudice and misinformation about these dogs. It was so bad that I mentioned it at a conference some time later. A genuinely concerned city official asked me for a copy of the letter so as to make sure it would not happen again; because he was obviously both sincere and well informed I agreed. I returned to my office in Leinster House and was taken aback to discover that the name at the bottom of the letter was that of the same concerned official! The moral is that you must confirm that the identified culprit is the real culprit.

Then, as a concerned citizen, ask to meet him or her. If you succeed, emphasise your independence: make it clear you are doing this yourself, because you are interested in travellers' rights, not because anyone on the site or working with the travellers who is employed by the local authority asked you. All this is necessary because there is a genuine fear that people can be victimised if they complain. (That explains the anonymity with which my account of the official and the guide dogs is described. The recipient of the letter, a prominent and well-respected figure in Dublin, was more than a little afraid that victimisation would follow any complaint.)

Once you have made contact with the official, ask why things are as they are. This can be a more difficult question than you might imagine. An acquaintance of mine, without water for almost a week and after numerous fruitless phone calls to his local authority, had to seek the assistance of a Government minister before he could find out who was supposed to be responsible for his water supply! But once you know you can ask awkward questions. Ask about environmental, sanitary and other standards that the local authority enforces elsewhere. If no progress is apparent, indicate that you are considering raising your concerns with the health board or with the Department of the Environment. That usually produces a predictable response that pressure will get you nowhere and that they are not going to be intimidated by threats such as that. And very often that's what quietens people down, or at least that and the vague promise of action in the future.

The reality is quite different. The last thing local officials want is detailed attention from the appropriate department. This is not because they are doing anything improper: it's just that it makes for more stress. It's also true that if the minister takes an interest then the civil servants will take an interest; and neither wants to be embarrassed. Therefore action will be requested. My conclusion is again that once the bluster about 'not giving in to pressure' begins, you can be sure you're making progress.

It is of course extremely important that you be both prepared and able to carry through your promise to pursue things. If you say you are going to pursue the matter then do so. As we will see below, a written Dáil question will usually get things moving.

There is much else happening locally. The local health board is not a secret body either. It publishes accounts. Ask your local library to get you a copy; look through them and see what you can learn. If you don't understand something, write and ask them. If that fails ask a member of the health board to try to find out for you. If that doesn't succeed then you could try a number of other angles. One would be to approach the local government auditor's office and query the accounts with them. They are conscientious public servants and will follow up your suggestion. And it would probably be worth your while to let the health board know you are doing that: it might improve attitudes!

Alternatively you can revert to your well-cultivated TD or senator. Ask the TD to put down written questions seeking the information you have been refused locally. You will almost invariably get it, and no matter how thick-skinned people appear to be they are in fact quite sensitive when information is made public. Information sought for me on the per capita costs of health board hostels around the country was accompanied by a detailed defence of the variation in costings from region to region, even though no such explanation was sought!

Make sure though that the TD also contacts the Department of Health and explains that the reason he or she has had to resort to a Dáil question is that the health board was reluctant to disclose the information. If they do that a few times then the local body will get a timely reminder from the department that they are causing a lot of department time to be wasted. A similar tactic can be used when you run into one of those public officials who believe that the best thing to do with incoming correspondence is to ignore it. Ask your cultivated TDs to put down a question to the Minister for Health asking for the information and also asking the minister to find out why the health board took so long to reply. And don't be afraid to do this again if practices don't improve. The first principle remains the same as before. If you want to find out, ask, and keep on asking.

There may be state agencies like FÁS or the IDA in your area about whom you wish to know more. All the information in the previous chapter will help you here again.

For other local bodies you will need a different approach. In the case of local schools it can depend on their ownership structure. This is usually the same for primary schools but can differ dramatically for second-level schools. All schools are supposed to have boards of management, but the boards' composition varies. Primary schools will, as we have seen, have two parents' representatives and a majority of 'patron's' representatives. If you want information find out the name and address of the individual members of the board, and ask them. They may feel bound by confidentiality, but it is important that you ask and are refused if you wish to pursue the matter further.

Remember that if they give you information that would otherwise be withheld, then the 'patron', usually a bishop, is under instructions to sack them from the board of management. Refusal is often the wiser course for them, particularly if they are direct nominees of the patron. In that event you have to move outside the formal structures. If it is a matter that you think would be important to parents generally then you could investigate the parents' association of the school. Ask them to look for the information. Ask them to ask for the school accounts or whatever you need. Most parents feel impotent and excluded; they are usually unaware of any way of raising matters that concern them with the school. They may want to do no more than complain about the quality of the tracksuits they are required to buy for their children or of the school overcoat, but they have no route for doing so. And however unreal it may appear, many parents are convinced that complaining does their children no good. The best route then is through the chairperson of the board of management, who is usually one of the local clergy. Don't just complain, ask for information. Find out how the suppliers are selected. Ask whether tenders were sought, and ask who vetted the tenders. And as before, always be prepared to take it further. Mention both the bishop and the Department of Education. Ask if there are specified procedures, and ask to see them. Ask members of the board for them; and if all else fails ask the Department of Education for them. As always, your final resort will be the written Dáil question, remembering to ask your helpful TD to let them know the reason they have to go through this procedure in order to get local information.

In the case of second-level schools there are a few points of detail that are different. Second-level schools are either fee-paying or non-fee-paying, with a further subdivision among the non-fee-paying schools. Some of these—the great majority of them—are private schools owned usually by religious orders, though the religious presence is not much in evidence nowadays. The chairperson of the board of management of one such school in Cork—who is the only member of the religious order involved with the school—lives at least a hundred miles from Cork. These schools have boards of management but are in effect still run by the religious and/or the principal. Their boards are set up by agreement with the department but are arguably even less accountable than those in primary schools. More accountable are the community schools, which are directly answerable to the Department of Education and are publicly owned. Their boards contain representatives of religious orders and local interests.

Finally there are the publicly owned and controlled schools. These ought to be the most accountable. Unfortunately, because of the competitive environment in which second-level schools operate, all schools have become secretive. Nevertheless it is worth trying to get some information.

If all else fails try a letter to your local papers. Ask parents who have had children go through the second-level system to contact you. Record their experiences of selection, of streaming, and of social mixing, and compile a report. Stick to the conclusions that the evidence sustains, and supply that to the newspapers. It will generate a response. This may be so great that it would be as well only to use information from parents whose children have left secondary school, because, as we've seen, there is still a widespread fear that criticism results in discrimination or in punitive action against the children. How else can one account for the silence of parents in Limerick for years in the face of the total secrecy that prevailed in the allocation of second-level places? Do they really think everyone was happy? Indeed the Limerick story confirms the usefulness of the approach I've suggested earlier. It was only when they got the minister involved that progress was made towards a resolution.

If you do turn up useful new information—and you will— remember to make it available. Local radio or newspapers rarely have the resources to go searching through Dáil records. Dáil and Seanad speeches are usually supplied by the maker of the speech, not by a reporter; so pass on your information to local journalists, and encourage them to use it. That will further add to the atmosphere of accountability that the country needs. And you will extend the interest of local journalists in the various ways in which it is possible to come upon information that ought to be published.

Other local information can be more difficult to determine. You may have difficulty finding out who exactly owns a local newspaper or local radio station. Local factories can often also be of indeterminate ownership, as in the case of Larry Goodman's companies cited earlier. (In a later chapter we'll have a look at various ways in which you can dig up information about businesses. This can also be useful if you're investigating local issues.)

Of course there are very few businesses that don't have employees, and fortunately a good proportion of these will be union members. In spite of the efforts of the EU, Irish employees have relatively little right to know about their employers. They have, however, a right to know a lot about the materials they handle and the premises they work in under the Health and Safety at Work Act. It's worth while, therefore, if you have concerns relating to environmental matters and the local authority is either indifferent or unhelpful to seek information from employees. Let them know that they are entitled to the information, and encourage them to ask. If something emerges by this route it may be enough to persuade a recalcitrant local authority to act. Useful and important concerns would relate to various solvents that are used for cleaning, degreasing, and the like, as well as the cleaning agents and detergents that might be used for sterilising and other purposes. These are often familiar substances, in use for years, but perhaps not properly accounted for in health and safety terms.

Health and safety legislation is wonderfully local in its application. It is designed to be implemented firm by firm, location by location, and the underlying policy of both the act and the authority that enforces it is to involve all employees in the pursuit of safety. So for a wide range of local concerns you could put it to great use. You shouldn't, however, expect too much from the authority itself. It is unfortunately infected with the culture of secrecy too.

13 MINDING THEIR BUSINESS

●●●●●●●●●●●●●●●●●●●●●●●

F inding out about the private sector is even more difficult than a similar investigation of the public sector. Nevertheless you can find out a lot. I recall a local controversy in the west of Ireland. A prominent and successful local businessman, a good employer, was objecting to a state development in his area. The community was divided on the issue, and it was asserted that the businessman-objector had 'never received a penny' from the state. This became part of the currency of the controversy, a controversy that generated much heat and left bad feelings in its wake. I was surprised to discover later that the records of the various development agencies showed that the businessman was not only a recipient of state aid but the biggest recipient in his area. And all that information was available from published sources.

Grants to individual companies are recorded in the national and regional reports of the IDA and Údarás na Gaeltachta. They're available in most public libraries and will give a local enquirer quite a lot of information about local business. Bord Fáilte's annual report will give similar information about grants for the tourist industry.

It's well worth while thinking about the Dáil question route again here. The private business sector is a major recipient of state funds and is also a major tax contributor. There is a massive volume of statistical information on the various sectors of the economy in the possession of Government departments. Various issues, such as the method of performance evaluation applied to monopolies (for example cable television services), are rarely pursued with any enthusiasm. Write out the questions you want answered, and ask a TD to submit them for you. It will save you an enormous amount of time and money, and may well unearth interesting new information.

If you suspect malpractice somewhere it's also worth pursuing the matter with a local TD. When they speak in the Dáil or Seanad, TDs and senators have absolute privilege: this means they can't be sued by anyone about anything they say there. If you have a convincing case but are worried about libel laws, then this route is worth pursuing.

There is a lot more that is accessible, though. The Companies Office in Dublin Castle is the best place to start. This office is meant to ensure that all companies that exercise the privilege of limited liability behave properly. This is necessary because, as we've seen, the privilege of limited liability is easily (and frequently) abused, even though it exists for the best of reasons, both business and social. It is this limited liability that has left so many people fuming when the builder whom they have contracted with goes bust, their deposit is lost, and yet the builder is visibly and sometimes ostentatiously unaffected by the collapse, retaining the big car and still taking the expensive holidays while the prospective home-owner has to accept the loss of thousands of pounds. Limited liability is a privilege instituted to enable people to limit their personal liabilities if a business venture goes wrong. The idea is to allow business people to expand and take risks without putting at risk any more of their personal assets than they initially choose. The alternative would be to leave a person's home and perhaps successful businesses threatened by greedy creditors or predatory banks.

This is fine as long as it extends only to the real hazards of business, but clever lawyers and unscrupulous people have unfortunately found many ways to siphon off money from a company before it collapses. Thus it often happens that when a company goes into liquidation, the creditors (people to whom money is owed, including those who have paid for but not received goods and services) find there is nothing left. Indeed experiences like this are so frequent that many suppliers will immediately, and without reference to the niceties of the law, repossess anything they have sold to a company once liquidation is announced.

This situation was apparently close to getting out of hand in the early 1980s when pressure from the EC (EU) forced the hand of the Government. The result is that the powers of the Companies Office and the obligations of companies have been significantly increased by recent legislation. Directors are now much more likely to be personally liable for a company's debts if there is evidence of recklessness on their part. There is also greater restriction on directors borrowing money from companies. And in certain circumstances people can be refused permission to form new companies or be required to commit a substantial amount of their personal assets to such a company.

Companies are obliged to make annual returns to the Companies Office, and in principle you should be able to get some idea of a company's performance from the office. This is the right of every citizen. You will be able to find out if the company is making its returns as required; you will find out the names of its directors, and perhaps some general information about its trading record; and details of any mortgages taken out in the name of the company are also available. But resolute stonewalling by successive Governments has left us with 'minimal disclosure' requirements. This was done, we were told, in the interests of 'small' companies so as to reduce their costs. This admirable concern left the great majority of companies safely shrouded in secrecy. Nevertheless the Companies Office is still worth a visit. If it turns out that the company you are interested in hasn't made returns, complain! It could provoke action that would save you and possibly other creditors from serious loss.

And of course company law doesn't just apply to businesses. Many voluntary and charitable groups are also, prudently and quite legitimately, limited companies. They are also required to make returns and supply details of their directors. Check if you are suspicious or need further information.

Financial institutions are required to make additional returns to the Central Bank. These should include any loans given at preferential rates to directors. But you won't get much out of the Central Bank: its commitment to the market economy, so eloquently put when it discusses issues such as social welfare and public expenditure, does not stretch to good consumer information. It is the Central Bank, after all, that allowed all the banks to deduct their multiple charges from our bank accounts with no or very limited explanation to us.

There are other ways of investigating ownership of property. The Land Registry can be a fruitful source of information, but it is expensive, and you'll probably need a lawyer to investigate it. More straightforward is the list of ratepayers held by every local authority. Everyone is entitled to inspect that, and it will let you know who the local authority believes is responsible for paying rates on every piece of business property in its jurisdiction. If it's information about landlords you're after then the register of electors ought to give you some idea of multiple occupancy. You can look at that in every post office and public library.

Most large urban local authorities have by-laws that are supposed to make every landlord register with them, though apparently the majority don't. Nevertheless an enquiry from a concerned citizen about a particular set of flats can often produce results. Even if the particular landlord isn't registered, your enquiry will probably propel the local authority into action. And of course conversion into flats requires planning permission. Check with the planning department. A repeated enquiry should once again move your local authority into action; if these don't work, ask a local councillor to intervene. If they can't or won't then it's back to the Dáil to ask a written question. Two good questions to ask together would be first to ask the Minister for the Environment how many landlords are registered with the local authorities of our cities; then ask the Minister for Social Welfare how many different people received supplementary welfare rent allowance in those areas during the same period; then ask a final question asking them to reconcile the figures!

More information on the private sector can be found in *Stubbs Gazette*. This specialised journal lists all judgments against companies and individuals who have been brought to court by their creditors. Much of that information is also a matter of record in the register of judgments in the High Court. Again you are entitled to inspect that.

You will also get additional information about a company when it seeks a stock market flotation. Both the law and the Stock Exchange require a considerable degree of transparency when a company seeks to persuade the general public to buy shares in it and those shares are to be traded on the Stock Exchange. It was under those circumstances, as we saw earlier, that the Irish Permanent Building Society abandoned its customary shyness and let us know a little about the rewards their senior executives believed they deserved. Nevertheless that information is a matter of permanent public record and gives a detailed insight into the otherwise secretive world of business.

There are other, less formal ways of finding out about the private sector. Trade unions are increasingly sophisticated in their dealings with employers, and informal contacts with the appropriate officials can provide useful information. They will usually have a good idea too about the company's trading performance. It's well worth the effort too to read through business and trade magazines in the local library; very often you'll dig up information that won't make it to the newspapers, or if it does it will usually only make it to the business pages. And the *Financial Times*, if you can get your hands on it, will often provide information that would be otherwise unavailable. It is always worth looking at magazines like *Consumer Choice* and *Which* as well. They are, in the present climate of secrecy, the only source of comparative evaluation of the performance of consumer goods.

Public limited companies (the ones that are quoted on the Stock Exchange) have to have annual general meetings, and all shareholders are entitled to attend and must be supplied with the companies' annual reports. These reports must contain audited accounts, and shareholders are entitled to ask questions at the AGM. So a group of concerned citizens, consumers, environmentalists or local residents near a smelly food or other factory, and indeed trade unionists, could make themselves very conspicuous if they bought shares in the offending company, attended the AGM, and asked all the questions they wanted.

One share would do it! There is no guarantee that all or indeed any of the answers would be provided, but the possible embarrassment would be a powerful incentive to the company. PLCs do not like to be embarrassed: it can affect the market's perceptions of them!

If you decide to buy a share, don't allow the atmosphere of grandiose cosiness that pervades most AGMs to intimidate you. It might be useful for a community group to register a number of people as owners of the shares so that a group can attend. Ask your questions, and insist on being answered. Point out that the company has legal obligations in health and safety, consumer and environmental law. Ask to be told which individual will be liable for penalties if the company is convicted. Remind them that a licence is not an excuse for pollution, though they may pretend it is.

Always remember that certain formalities have to be dealt with at these AGMs. The board of directors have to be selected, though this is usually a formality. Oppose the re-election of the board if you don't get satisfactory information. You'll be overwhelmingly defeated, but you'll have made your point. Indeed if it's a large PLC you're dealing with there will be a few journalists there; bring along some information for them too. It's useful to know what sections of environmental, safety and other legislation are appropriate. Pass that on to the journalists present.

Actions like this would be useful in a number of areas. You could ask the two large banks about their treatment of their customers and staff. Ask them how they hope to win customer support with a demoralised work force. You could ask for a precise breakdown of the amount of money made from currency speculation in the previous year. With a bit of background reading you could enquire about 'hedging' funds. These are funds that the institutions keep and use to minimise the risk of exchange and other losses; they are now so big that they can undermine powerful currencies, not to mention the poor old Irish pound. Ask them if they have any position on the environmental policy of companies they lend to; point out that in the United States such institutions are probably going to have to pay the bills for cleaning up the environmental mess caused by companies they supported. How will that affect their shares?

The environmental record of the various food processing companies that have become PLCs in recent years would be worth investigating. The Keystone Cops flavour of one such company's efforts to evade its environmental responsibilities was detailed in the High Court some years ago. That might have been clever in the short term but could damage the company and its shareholders in the long run. Not unrelated to that might be queries about donations to political parties; indeed the fact that the disclosure of such donations is not compulsory underlines our institutional indifference to accountability.

It's also always worth enquiring about the remuneration and gratuities of the board. Ask particularly about the chief executive and also about the non-executive directors. Ask how many days they work. Don't forget to enquire about share options. These are a clever device whereby 'important' people are given an option on a certain number of shares at a given price. They don't have to pay anything for them, though; then if the company does well the value of the shares in the option increases, and, when it suits, the option holder can dispose of the shares at the new, higher price. He or she then pays back the original price fixed for the shares and takes the profit, without having had to spend a penny.

Of course most of the above is only possible when dealing with Irish companies; multinationals would require a different strategy. They will have AGMs too, but usually in the country of their head office, and seekers after information can't afford to travel to New York or Frankfurt to ask questions at an AGM. Nevertheless it's worth trying to get questions asked, because disclosure regulations are more demanding in the United States and Germany, and even in Britain, than they are here. In addition multinationals are concerned to be regarded as good corporate citizens in their home country, while at the same time they are usually under pressure from environmental and consumer groups at home. Their shareholders too tend to be much more assertive than their Irish counterparts. The withdrawal of many American companies from South Africa was as much a result of shareholder and consumer pressure as it was a response to political pressure. So if you have concerns about safety, environmental or other matters, try contacting activists in these countries.

Check up a bit to see if legislation in the home country is more stringent than here: it may well be that information that is withheld here will have to be disclosed at home. Check too if you're dealing with an American company about local as distinct from federal requirements. A good place to start if you are looking for information in the United States is with the Center for National Security Studies in Washington (phone 001 202 5445380). Their publications record both their successes and failures. They can also supply you with information about other groups worth dealing with.

These pressures can produce results, but they require stamina and effort. The names of consumer organisations can be got from the Consumers' Association, of trade unions from the ICTU, and of environmental organisations from Greenpeace or similar organisations. Assemble your information carefully first. The IDA will tell you what the parent company of any multinational is, for instance. Sort out what it is you want to know: is it environmental information, or policy, consumer concerns, safety issues, or employment practices? Write to the appropriate organisations, and you will often be surprised by the response. They will often help you to find the best source of the information. And remember that the Freedom of Information Act is not just available to US citizens. It is, as we will see, a powerful but slow weapon.

Finally, if you are concerned about information on the private or indeed any other sector that operates internationally, you cannot avoid dealing with computers. They are the primary tool in the transfer of information and in gaining access to stored information. They are also relatively cheap, and can link you into some of the data-bases prepared by organisations all round the world as well as in Ireland. All you need is a relatively modern desktop computer, a telephone line, a device called a modem, and the appropriate software. With that much in place buy a copy of any of the main computer magazines and look for articles about communications; they will explain how to get started. In particular find out about the Internet, the international network of computers. This will enable you to access computers all round the world while only paying local telephone charges. Internet access is available to private users for £10–15 per month. Once you are over the initial learning period you can start writing to various groups around the world that have data-bases of information. Some of these are commercial, some are non-profit.

Again it's worth while contacting interest groups in the United States and Britain as a starting point. From them you can find out what's available. Then you can use your own computer, via the telephone line, to search for information. The telephone call charges are relatively low, particularly if you take advantage of the reduced rate (after six o'clock and at weekends). If you are searching for information on a particular company then a computer search will take only a few seconds; and if the records are available it can be quite cheap to have them transferred to your own computer. It's often better to identify the title of the document from the computer and then follow up with a request through your local library for a copy of the relevant articles. You'll have to pay for this, but it may be cheaper than having the documents transferred to you over the telephone connection. It shouldn't amount to more than postage and photocopying, plus a small handling charge.

All this means that it is possible by dint of hard work to find out more than the corporate sector would want us to know. Unfortunately other sectors of society that are ostensibly open, such as the Catholic Church and the trade unions, are a good deal more difficult to penetrate. The church in particular seems to believe it has to give an appearance of absolute unanimity on every issue, and seems determined, either by deliberate choice or by inertia, not to budge from that position. The frustration this generates for church members is indescribable, as a survey conducted by the Augustinians a few years ago showed. People felt alienated and excluded; they knew that no-one really listened to them and that their active involvement in the church, so much talked about, really meant that more people should become lay readers, distribute communion, and help out with voluntary organisations. Attempts to penetrate further into the institutional church were met with a velvet-covered but immovable barrier, epitomised by the continuing absence of any elected forum where the voice of lay people could be heard. Most church-going Catholics have given up on the bishops, who blissfully or foolishly confuse apathy with acceptance.

If you are in the minority who care and want to find out what's going on, you will, as in so many other areas, have to start outside Ireland. The *Tablet*, the British Catholic weekly, will provide you with more information on goings-on in the church than most of the Catholic publications produced in Ireland together. This is because most of the Irish publications start from the extraordinary presumption that whatever the bishops, and even more so the Pope, say is correct, even when they contradict themselves or duck the consequences of their statements. And if there is disagreement they ignore it too.

Still, it's worth making the effort, for a number of reasons. Begin by asking your local clergy to publish the parochial accounts. This might be in their own interests too, because many priests survive on abysmally small incomes; if they actually told the whole story people would, as they always do, respond generously. It's well worth while too telling priests what you think of sermons and Mass in your parish. Then contact the local bishop and ask to meet him. Say you're interested in his thoughts on the role of the laity in the church. Persist in looking for a meeting. Remind him that in other countries lay people are centrally involved in policy planning, organisation, and so on. Ask him why it's different here. Ask him whom he talks to about important issues. Suggest a more open, participative structure. When he demurs refer to other countries. From the *Tablet* you'll have discovered that in other countries independent lay people have a major role. Why not here? Arm yourself with information, because the first line of defence within the clerical church is denial. Ask why the Irish Catholic Church, unlike its counterparts in England, Scotland, and Wales, demurs from formally accepting the title 'Roman Catholic' (the official excuse is that it would upset the laity, whose capacity to be upset was discovered presumably by a close inspection of the bishops' hearts). Ask him why in Ireland inter-church marriages are more tightly regulated than in Alsace-Lorraine in France or other places. Ask him why he doesn't set up a formal elected representative structure for the laity in his diocese. His excuse will be that nobody seems to want to get involved; explain that it's difficult for all but the most determined or the most servile to accept a form of participation that involves being required to leave your brain and your professional and personal skills outside the door! Persist. I am convinced that bishops collectively and individually believe they are doing a good job, because no-one from within the church bothers to say anything to them.

Finally there is that other pillar of privacy, the trade union movement. This is of course ostensibly a model of democracy, with all decisions ultimately in the hands of the membership, and a leadership that is always accountable to that membership. It is in fact heavily controlled, hierarchical, and centralised. Indeed it is a mirror image of the state itself, and, somewhat ironically, reflects the institutional stamp of the Catholic Church with its suspicion of accountability. Observation of the operation of an ICTU annual conference will confirm this. This is the body that determines overall trade union policy, policy that is meant to be implemented by the Congress executive. Observe there the dual role played by members of the executive, usually full-time officials of their own unions, who spend as much time on the floor ensuring that their own delegations don't raise any awkward motions or ask any awkward questions as they do on the platform representing the executive. ICTU conferences end up being little more than electoral gatherings dominated by the determination of the bureaucracy to be re-elected to the executive; the rest is window-dressing.

If you want to find out more, it's virtually impossible if you're not a member of a union. If you are, your local trades council is a good place to start. Try to get yourself elected as a delegate to that body, and become an active participant there. The competition usually won't be that demanding. Then you can raise issues that deserve an airing at ICTU conferences. This approach can be particularly useful, because delegates from trades councils are not under the thumb of their union officials and can often act and speak independently.

Failing that, it's worth keeping an eye on your local papers to find the names of prominent trade union activists in your area. These activists are often thorns in the side of their own officials, and in most cases enjoy their role. Try them out if you want issues raised or pursued within the movement. Ask that the issues be aired at union meetings. You may find a ready response!

14 INVESTIGATING THE INVESTIGATORS

● ●

'I think newspapers are out of touch. There's been a huge drift away from the hard news type of journalism and into commentary ... An awful lot of what passes for journalism nowadays could be written without ever having contact with real people ... If journalism is to be perceived as just polished writers sounding off about something, you don't even have to get out of bed in the morning. Seriously.' (Damien Kiberd, editor, *Sunday Business Post*, quoted by Ivor Kenny in *Talking to Ourselves: Conversations with Editors of the Irish News Media*, Kenny, Galway, 1994.)

The emphasis in this book so far has been on the individual's struggle to get access to information, both from the public and the private sector. That emphasis on struggle corresponds to my own experience and, I'm sure, reflects reality. Nevertheless it is not a reality that seems to perturb many in our society.

This comes as a surprise at first. When I published and introduced my own Freedom of Information Bill, I remembered the publicity and fuss that attended earlier private members' legislation such as Mary Robinson's first Family Planning Bill, or indeed my own Homeless Persons Bill. Since we have what is described as a free press, which, we are assured, is not only guaranteed but jealously guards the right to report on all matters not covered by the laws of libel, the Official Secrets Act, or the now limited censorship laws, I expected a reasonable degree of interest. It would be thought that in an era of increasingly powerful government, with an array of ever more complex regulations, the clamour to know what is going on would be loud, sustained, and irresistible. Many 'important' people in the media had written and pronounced in various forums and summer schools about our overwhelming secretiveness. I was disappointed. Indeed coverage of the debate in the Seanad was about on a par with that given to the routine discussion of potholes, school building programmes, and the like. And that was only in a couple of newspapers. No-one else noticed.

Wounded vanity is a great stimulus! As I reflected I realised that even without new legislation we ought to be enjoying a feast of information: company records, Dáil questions, searches of the National Archives, and so on. The increasing scale of government, the rising level of community involvement in environmental matters, parental involvement in schools and the claim that the Irish newspaper market is the most competitive in the world should have guaranteed that. Unfortunately it didn't; information didn't have the appeal it once had. Searching for the truth had slipped down the agenda. I had clearly misunderstood the media. In particular I hadn't noticed the way they had changed.

It's probably next to impossible to prove all this, but I have been forced to the conclusion that most of the media are engaged in what amounts to a systematic retreat from their information-giving role. In that role their objectives were clear: they were there to inform and indeed often provoke their readers. Nowadays they appear to prefer a painless entertainment role, coupled with a propaganda role in which they regurgitate material supplied by the Government and its agencies. Part of that entertainment role appears to involve a considerable effort to ensure that the preoccupations and indeed prejudices of their target audiences are massaged, often amplified, and rarely if ever challenged. How else does one explain, for instance, the preoccupation of the *Irish Times* with a policy measure as minuscule as the residential property tax? It must be a response to the preoccupations of the more vocal of their Dublin readership. For what other reason could a newspaper with pretensions to be a newspaper of record choose to make such an insignificant tax change the leading item in its 1994 budget supplement?

A quick look at any of the national papers and a comparison with twenty years ago adds to this impression. Detailed reporting of the issues of the day and the great needs of the day have been replaced by expanded opinion columns, expanded arts and culture coverage, enormously expanded sports coverage, and a plethora of supplements, the most prominent being the property supplements. As additional material all these might be welcome; but when they replace real news then we have reason to complain.

What we tend to have are large numbers of 'experts' writing large amounts explaining their *interpretation* of what has happened (almost overwhelmingly from a similar political perspective) or speculating on what is going to happen. There will be long interviews with figures of note in the arts, culture, and related spheres. These notabilities will also give us the benefit of their wisdom and authority on the state of the world generally. Opinions will extend well beyond the area of expertise that they may have, but by and large they will reflect the perceived preferences of the target audience. Unfortunately, while all this may well provide extra entertainment, little of it provides extra information. Regular listeners to radio news programmes will recognise this phenomenon too: lots of well-rounded words from an endless list of 'commentators', but not much more *information* than used to fit into the old ten-minute news bulletins.

And of course many issues are just left out. There's no conspiracy or anything like that involved; but there is a conviction that some stories (e.g. the North) are boring, and there is also the convenience of having a large volume of one side of the argument supplied by the small number of news agencies that dominate world news-gathering. And they still have to find space for the acres of commentary, opinion and 'colour' that are apparently felt necessary to sell papers today.

Also in evidence is a gradual debasement of language, particularly evident in the carefully polished adjectival revisions of the 1980s. What's left of the Communist Party in Russia are happily referred to as 'conservatives', for instance. In fact until the arrival of Zhirinovski they were also, with cavalier indifference to history, usually referred to as 'right-wingers'! By contrast, those who, in Russia, under the tutelage of the IMF and World Bank are attempting the most dramatic experiment in laissez-faire market economics in history are described as 'reformers', or even 'liberals'. Language was turned inside out.

Equally indicative is the language used in Britain. Margaret Thatcher led the most right-wing government that Britain had had for perhaps fifty years. Large sections of the Conservative Party disagreed with her. In conventional politics such people would be regarded as centrists or even of the left. Mrs Thatcher would have been happy to call them just that—she was, after all, happy to be branded an extremist; her media allies, however, liked her too much for that, and indeed many of them felt uncomfortable with a position on the right of the political spectrum. It was convenient for all concerned, therefore, if all those of the left and centre of the Tory party were instead branded as 'wets', a finely chosen pejorative term.

Mrs Thatcher's efforts were perceived to be so successful that it was felt that the Labour Party had to change its position too. Since this was clearly a good thing, those in Labour who took that view were labelled 'modernisers' or 'moderates', with the clear implication that the rest were a crowd of 'extremists'. What else can you be if you're not a 'moderate'?

These myths were not just pursued in Britain: many of the labels were imported into Ireland. The struggles in the Labour Party in the 1980s were conveniently presented as a struggle between 'the left' and 'the moderates', so that we all knew what point on the political spectrum 'the left' occupied. At the same time learned commentator after learned commentator eulogised the advances made for 'free market' economics in Britain under Thatcherism. The eulogies extended to glowing praise for the extension of 'freedom of choice' in Britain in the same era. The state was being rolled back decisively; the individual was supreme. 'Extremists', some significant and well known like Ken Livingstone, others more obscure, were occasionally heard to mention the increasing censorship of that period, the undermining of local government and increasingly secretive centralisation that took place. Indeed the public sector in Britain all through the Thatcher years was proportionately larger than in Ireland. Only 'extremists' worried about the decline in industrial production in Britain. They were ignored here. We had our model, and we were urged to follow.

This was the decade of the Reagan-Thatcher understanding. One of the products of that understanding was a determination to 'deal with terrorism'. This 'good thing' was much approved of both in Ireland and abroad. Those who 'used violence to achieve political ends' were to be purged. And again it was only 'extremists' like John Pilger and Noam Chomsky who wondered about the hypocrisy involved in the use of those words by governments that provided military and political support for the Khmer Rouge and fomented political violence in Nicaragua, Angola, and Mozambique, while organising brutal repression in El Salvador and Guatemala. Language was surely debased when an Irish parliament, ostensibly hostile to political violence, gave a standing ovation to Ronald Reagan, the author of political violence in places as far apart as Nicaragua, Mozambique, and Cambodia. Noam Chomsky observed that even liberal America accepted Reagan's agenda on Central America. They didn't like his crude violence, but his right to try to overthrow a government he didn't like was never challenged.

Facts, it appeared all through the 1980s, could not be allowed to interfere with the rhetoric. Facts, particularly economic facts, are boring and colourless (as in 'I don't want to bore you with statistics'). Altogether more colourful is a new and less taxing role for the media, with the emphasis on subjective perceptions, well written but with only a limited reference to reality and an obligatory tone of frivolity or else of personal abuse. That pursuit of entertainment finds ample material in politics, of course: the tortuous nature of political decision-making and the inevitable compromises between aspiration and reality are material enough. The carry-on of individual members of the political classes adds to the value. So you *will* find colourful and usually well-written accounts of incidents at question time in the Dáil or the order of business, usually supplemented with extracts from a supplied script or two (even though only members of the Government are supposed to use scripts in the Dáil or Seanad). 'Serious' newspapers will supplement this with what has become the central feature of what is left of political reportage (as distinct from political commentary): this is the sketch in which the clever writer paints an entertaining word-picture of an incident or two. Information will be distinctly hard to find.

All this is topped off by a studied cynicism. This was shown very clearly by the editor of the *Sunday Independent*—a newspaper with serious intellectual pretensions—in an interview with *Hot Press*. Asked to identify humanity's most useless invention, he replied with what he obviously believed to be devastating wit, 'Politics.' Cynicism is of course the response of the defeated, and, like that editor, political journalists seem to have been battered into such a defeated cynicism by the increasingly sophisticated PR machine of governments. How often do you see a political correspondent break a major story, for instance? Perhaps the biggest of recent years, Emily O'Reilly's publication of a draft of the Government position on Northern Ireland, resulted in the Gardaí being called! This was a political position paper, not a security document, but outrage was universal, and threatening.

For many, the alternative route of the off-the-record briefing is the preferred option. This gives the public the impression that they are being told something and the journalists the impression that they are important, so it works well for everyone. The only trouble is that it leaves the supply of information under the control of the Government.

Journalists who are involved with politics like to affect an air of informed detachment. They are, after all, frequently called upon to explain complex matters to the rest of us. It's a surprise therefore to discover, as I did, the extent to which attitudes are more a reflection of the predilections of the liberal minority at the centre of Irish life than the product of learning or life experiences. All through the eighties, for instance, most journalists unquestioningly accepted the prescriptions of a small but vocal group of economists. These prescriptions included a demand for reduced taxes, reduced public expenditure, and so on. They were based, we were told, on 'the laws of the market' or, even more grandiosely, 'the laws of economics'. The successes of Reaganism and Thatcherism were held up as unchallengeable evidence to this effect. And our media swallowed it all. Only one economic correspondent dissented from the chorus: that was Colm Rapple, who registered his dissent in the columns of the *Irish Independent*.

Many people outside the media knew that the 'facts' that were being used to advance the new orthodoxy were at best highly selective and at worst deliberately deceptive. Much was made of Reagan's tax cuts, for instance, and it took the Irish media ten years to discover that in fact average working people ended up paying more taxes under Reagan: it was the well-off who got the tax breaks. And of course it was no different in Ireland. 'Objective' analysis of the 'tax burden' led to demands for a reduction in the top rate of tax; the fact that the authors and publicists of such a reduction would be major beneficiaries was conveniently not adverted to. It was equally taken as factual that the problems with the public finances were caused by the 1977–81 Fianna Fáil Government. Simply noting the fact that our problems with public expenditure took off when the banks and their allies persuaded Governments to raise interest rates above the rate of inflation would have helped public debate considerably. All we were told was that this was meant to curb inflation. The fact that banks and the wealthy were made rich at the expense of the rest of us was conveniently left out of the discussion.

And as the entertainment and the orthodoxies took over, those boring details known as the facts were let slide further out of view. Reporting of the business of the Oireachtas became less and less visible in all the newspapers as political gossip took up more and more space. The committee stage of major legislation, dealing with issues as disparate as the rights of children, the environment, and company law, was conducted in front of largely empty press galleries.

This was easy to understand, even if impossible to justify. The Dáil correspondents rarely understood the discussion, the political correspondents were increasingly above all that, and the newspapers and other media didn't really think it worth the while of their specialist correspondents following such debates. After all, they could always rely on the very efficient Government press service to keep them informed. And of course the Government obliged, when it suited. It came as no surprise to me therefore to find that doctors didn't know that the Clinical Trials Bill was almost rewritten during its passage through the Dáil and Seanad, as was the Status of Children Bill, or that child care lobbyists were often ignorant of major amendments to the Children's Act. Indeed I know that the employees of one health board, given the job of implementing the Children's Act, were setting out to implement the unamended version! And all this happened during what we were told was an information explosion.

When media interest in such a central concern as legislation is so slight it is no surprise when the marginalised in our society are dismissed with what amounts to a metaphorical wave of the hand. How many of the commentators have ever thought of what they're actually saying when they talk about 'incentives' and more particularly 'incentives to work'. That phrase, much beloved of economists, floats around every conversation, debate and analysis of unemployment. It is assumed that 'disincentives' exist and cause people not to take up jobs. Much is written about the policy changes that are needed to 'restore incentives.' What a pity then that one rarely if ever finds much reference to even the published facts in the organs of the 'free press'. Information on the numbers of jobs that went unfilled because of the 'disincentive effect' associated with both our welfare and our tax systems would help us along. None was ever provided. Increasingly it appeared that the poor were fair game, though I'm sure that most editors would deny that with an impressive level of outrage. Long articles appeared in which it was asserted that hundreds of millions of pounds was being stolen in welfare abuse; evidence to justify this assertion was difficult to come by, but didn't deter the columnists. After all, they had the 'laws' of economics on their side!

Other media presumptions have become so universal that you have to remind yourself to ask for the evidence. I remember that model of the modern liberal Irishman, Dr Anthony Clare, professing himself 'astonished' when he discovered that over 80 per cent of Irish people go to church every Sunday. Of course he was astonished: hadn't all the media been telling him for years about 'declining levels of church-going'! 'I mean, everybody knew …' 'I mean, hardly anyone I know ever …' 'I mean …'

It's much the same with two other organisations of substance: Fianna Fáil and the GAA. In a perceptive, inquisitive media culture, surely someone would have commented on the fact that the FAI cup final in Dublin could only attract ten thousand people, while the same number attended a first-round Leinster GAA match between two teams that had virtually no hope of winning anything. Could the failure to notice the contrast be anything to do with commercial sponsorship and the need to keep advertisers happy?

Perhaps their denials even extend to what they write in their property supplements. These, it is supposed, give the potential purchaser enormous amounts of information. And they do, because they contain a lot of advertising! But look over what is written in those supplements, usually by serious journalists. You can't help noticing how lucky we are. After all, there never seems to be a bad buy in the property market. Has anyone ever seen a piece in a property supplement that was other than positive, or even eulogistic? All developments are selling well and represent great opportunities for first-time purchasers, or for the more mature, or whoever. There are no bad buys about, apparently; or if there are, the property supplement writers don't seem to know about them.

The media have a problem here. They are well aware of the increasing concern for the environment among the much sought-after ABC1 sections of society. They have expanded their environmental coverage to reflect that, and much is written about the environmental problems of our cities. Many media commentators have put together worthwhile ideas about, for instance, restricting the rights of car users in order to improve the urban environment. Many of them too are well informed on the chemical industry and its effluents. They will acknowledge the concerns of millions about global warming; but such concerns will never throw a shadow over the glowing rhetoric of the property pages.

Even less so will they visit the business pages, where orthodox dogma is all-powerful.

There are other reasons to be concerned about this blurring of the boundary between information and propaganda. The most significant, I believe, has been the decision of Governments in recent years to use public funds to promote one particular side of the argument in referendums. Before the referendum on the Single European Act, public funds were not used to seek a particular outcome; for that referendum the convention was abandoned, and money extracted compulsorily from citizens was used to persuade them to change their Constitution. Almost no-one objected. Everyone in the media knew that 'Europe' was a 'good thing'; debate was not needed on that.

This exercise was repeated during the referendum on Maastricht, and again only a few, most notably Patricia McKenna, objected. Finally, as I write, the Government has announced that it will be using public funds to persuade people to vote 'yes' for divorce, and the liberals are silent. And of course they were silent too when the Taoiseach used his powers to commandeer time on RTE to urge a 'yes' vote on Maastricht. RTE, sycophantic as always, having been bullied once by the Government, promptly repeated the imposed speech in its immediately following nine o'clock news. Not an eyebrow was raised among the media community.

Just how far down this propaganda road will Governments have to go before the media rediscover their role? Indeed it may not even end there. One very prominent liberal has assured me that RTE will never again, on a European referendum, give equal time in current affairs discussions to both sides of the argument. But of course RTE has a way of dealing with these things. One senior executive there justified their non-coverage of Indonesian genocide in East Timor on the grounds that their viewers didn't know anything about East Timor!

Regrettably, therefore, it appears that the information explosion has turned into a propaganda victory for the Government and business. They can saturate the willing media with plentiful but harmless quasi-propaganda while keeping significant information under lock and key. They can dictate the agenda and ensure that whole issues and ranges of ideas are left out. And they are quite comfortable with their position. Only a revolution in accountability can reverse it. We will look at the essential features of such a revolution in the following chapters.

Part 4
An End to All That: Proposals for Reform

15 A REVOLUTION OF LIGHT

● ●

What is proposed in the next few chapters sounds revolutionary. Nevertheless, either hypocritically or paradoxically, it would, at least in part, be formally welcomed by many in Irish life. Huge and influential sections of Irish society have already expressed their support.

When my own Freedom of Information Bill was debated in the Seanad, everyone was in favour of it! Spokespersons for Fine Gael and the Labour Party were enthusiastically in favour. A minister of state, Noel Treacy, was also very positive, though he of course wanted us to leave it all to the Government. Nevertheless the principle was accepted. Indeed the only serious criticism of my bill that he could offer was a suggestion that exam papers might not be as secure as they should be!

The Association of Higher Civil Servants made their support for freedom of information known as far back as October 1985, in a submission to an Oireachtas committee. Their submission is brief and to the point; it adverts to almost all the issues of concern that we will be dealing with in the next chapter. The Irish Council for Civil Liberties has long campaigned for this and other institutional changes, as has the Consumers' Association of Ireland. We've had demands too, at least occasionally, from some sections of the media, and in recent years there have been academic seminars about the issue.

And we're not alone in this. There has been an increasing

demand for legislation on access to information in Britain. That demand has been, ironically, resisted both by Mrs Thatcher and her successor. The irony arises from the fact that Mrs Thatcher and her ally in the United States were both ostensibly dedicated to maximising the power of the individual and reducing the power of the state; but this didn't inhibit either from attempting in every way possible to increase secrecy and reduce accountability. Both of them, for instance, struggled to make it impossible for anyone to lawfully disclose secret law-breaking by the state.

And yet I remain convinced that in practice, and perhaps covertly, any radical change in disclosure of information would meet with resistance from almost every influential section of society. It's inevitable then that, in tandem with appropriate but measured support, a host of objections will be raised. Few of these will be directly negative. Instead they will, as we'll see, range from the patronising (the 'well-intentioned but naïve' dismissal) through the suspicious ('need to avoid undermining the state') to the worldly-wise and cynical ('good idea but nobody's interested'). Within that framework every possible objection is cited, from the defamation laws through the need for people to be able to express themselves freely to the laughable but widely used argument that the preparatory work required (indexing of documents, for example) would be so enormous as to make any generally applicable freedom of information legislation impossible to implement. (The vision this conjures up of our institutions swamped in a sea of disorganised, unindexed paper seems to me to represent current reality quite well. Freedom of information would then be doing no more than requiring them to reach a level of efficiency that would be normal in any large organisation. What do they want all those records for if they aren't even indexed?)

And of course even if the principle is still accepted, large and broadly worded exemptions will be proposed, to be followed in turn by an administrative regime that is as generous as possible to the holders of information. Even with that they will then find ways to slow down the process.

We will deal with the objectors and inhibitors later. Let's state our principle first: 'All records in the possession of the state and its agencies, both national and local, should be accessible to the public for inspection and copying, save for a number of clearly delineated exceptions.' If you try that on your local TD, or indeed on many a local and national bureaucrat, they'll tell you it's a great idea and then trip you up in quibbles, queries, and diversions. Apart from the more ludicrous general objections, which we've already mentioned, others will surface.

The object of the rest of this book, therefore, is to equip the reader to both support the demand for freedom of information, or more precisely for a functioning democracy, and to deal with all the objections, quibbles, and diversions.

It does appear that almost everyone is officially in favour of freedom of access to information. Indeed it is easy to pillory those few who honestly state their objections as being almost eccentric. Politicians, particularly when they are out of office, civil servants and media people all recognise the importance of information in a 'modern democracy'. We end up with the peculiar situation where it appears that while everyone who has any influence supports reform, nothing has been done about it.

Even the apparently contrasting attitudes of the present and preceding Governments seem to me to confirm the inertial slowness of reform. The previous Government promised to 'consider' the introduction of a Freedom of Information Act. I've no idea why that form of words was chosen, but it did underline the resistance to change that still remains. The present Government under John Bruton is committed to introducing a Freedom of Information Act. It is full of the rhetoric of transparency. And it is all most welcome. Except that of course there is nothing to prevent them making most of the documentation that would obviously be covered by freedom of information legislation available immediately to the public even before the legislation is published. They could also direct various state agencies to operate both the spirit and the letter of the Freedom of Environment Information Directive referred to earlier. Or they can wait and 'consult' us!

So if we propose specific actions we will get the ritual response that the matter is 'under consideration', as it has been since an Oireachtas committee first considered it in the early 1980s. Why 'consideration' has taken the best part of ten years is worth exploring, and there is no shortage of 'respectable' interpretations. My own interpretation, the fruit of twelve years observing the attitudes and priorities of our political, bureaucratic and, not least, media establishments, is not so 'respectable'.

An obvious reason for the sloth and inertia is the absence of demand for reform from 'significant' circles of our society (occasional appropriate remarks should not be confused with demands). The Oireachtas, for instance, one possible centre for the making of such demands, is in effect under the control of the Government (even though the Constitution suggests that that relationship should be reversed). Within that framework of control, Government TDs and senators can find out as much as they are allowed to know by the various informal routes we discussed earlier. But because they are under such firm control they won't push too hard when disapproval is expressed. Opposition members will of course espouse freedom of information but are often happy enough with the status quo. This leaves them as the conduits, providers and monopolisers of access when it comes to information. All back-bench members are either so politically castrated or so comfortable with the status quo that they rarely act independently; so comfortable are they with their role as intermediaries that they even have a vested interest in the actual inhibition of reform.

It is true of course that demand for reform is not the exclusive preserve of the Oireachtas. We are a democracy, after all. Individual citizens, academics, pressure groups and the media can all exercise their right to free speech and demand reform. And some of them do. The problem is that in the current climate, where matters economic are identified as the first and overwhelming priority, followed closely by what are ambiguously called 'social' reforms, institutional reform gets squeezed out. Nevertheless it is difficult to overstate the almost total failure of either our intellectual or media authorities to identify the links between economic performance (and indeed 'social change') and institutional reform.

Part of this is explicable by something we referred to earlier: the dominant position occupied by economists in our political process. In the opinion of an increasing number of commentators, it is a somewhat simplistic view to let debate on the future direction of the country be dominated by (mostly academic) economists. Most of them adhere to a single model of economic development, though the level of agreement is usually clouded by vigorous argument about details. We are almost uncritically presented then with the quaintly simplistic model of society to which most economists cling. In that view all state institutions are a bad thing, and therefore the solution is not reform but abolition. The singular view is further reinforced when your perception of 'good' economic policy amounts to no more than minimising the 'interference' of the state in the 'market'. This is particularly easy if you believe that welfare is largely an inhibitor of the market, publicly provided health a source of inefficiency, and state education a deterrent to performance. Most of our high-profile economists believe all this, and they therefore have a wonderfully simplistic alternative. They advocate greater 'competition' via privatisation, market testing, or whatever phrase is fashionable.

There are, of course, many economists and even larger numbers of ordinary people who disagree with them. (How many of us, for instance, really believe that the average person would prefer never to work at all? Most economists do!) But unfortunately there are filters on what we are allowed to read and see. These filters are controlled by people—newspaper editors in particular—who happily, and apparently uncritically, give their allegiance to this 'market' version of human behaviour. They will pretend to be objective, but since institutional reform has neither the slightly racy ring of what is described as 'social' reform nor the terror that goes with violence, nor the advertising power of business, it's squeezed out as a day-to-day topic. Contrast the newspapers' concern with reform of the libel laws with their concern for freedom of information! All this means that those who masquerade as our 'thinkers' and those who interpret them for us see no future in institutional reform.

The second great reason for the contrast between theory and action is related to the nature of our democracies. As we'll see, the most liberal freedom of information laws have developed in the United States and Sweden. One is a global power, the other a small, rich neutral state. Sweden's position is perhaps related to its early development of democratic institutions and the popular commitment to them. The situation in the United States arose from a revolt by the Congress against the abuses of power by the executive, particularly in the late 1960s and early 1970s. The present relatively effective form of the Freedom of Information Act was passed by the Congress in 1976, when it overturned a veto by the then president. Its relative success has produced a response, of course. Successive presidents have attempted to have the most effective sections of that Act neutralised and diluted. Where that has failed they have used executive orders to minimise their effect.

All this should be a warning to us, and because it is we will discuss at length later the various devices that have been used. All of them will certainly be used here to either prevent or emasculate freedom of information legislation.

But already we can identify a common thread. It is as if the government in virtually every one of what are called the democracies is apparently convinced or chooses to believe that the very survival of democracy depends on the state being allowed to be as undemocratic as the government feels is necessary. That this is a contradiction goes without saying; nevertheless this superficially obvious contradiction serves a useful purpose: it conceals the more obscure but more sinister contradiction that underlies all this. That is the suspicion that a large part of our state apparatus doesn't believe in government of the people, for the people, and by the people, because it is apparently convinced that the people aren't really able to understand the great issues that need to be disposed of. This may not actually be the case, but the language used and the tone the discussion takes suggest that many of those who control and influence our lives are not as clear on the fundamentals of democracy as we would assume!

This less than healthy attitude to democracy surfaces in public from time to time, but it suits many in our centres of power to minimise attention to it. It surfaces, for instance, when the 'democratic deficit' in the European institutions is discussed. There is usually a lot of well-intentioned talk about the 'need to increase participation' or the 'need to reduce secrecy', or the need to 'give ordinary Europeans a greater say in the determination of policy.' All of these are seen as manifestations of idealism, of the desire to build the 'new Europe'. The peculiarity of the underlying assumption is rarely noticed. This is that 'they' are going to be persuaded or asked to allow 'us' to participate in the decisions that change our lives: 'we' are going to be allowed to share in the power that 'they' have. Now this is peculiar, because it appears to assume the existence of political power that does not arise from the sovereignty of the people. Such power contradicts the first principle of democracy. In a democracy 'we' allow 'them' to exercise power on our behalf and with our consent. We are the source of power, and they are our servants. Much of the European talk seems to assume the existence of a power independent of us that is now to be asked nicely to share a little of it with us.

Further evidence of this emerged when the European Union made a tentative move in the direction of freedom of access to information with its Directive on Information on the Environment. Most recently the EU has attempted to underline its democratic credentials with a declaration on Freedom of Access to Information from the Council of Ministers in 1993.

This declaration was taken literally by the *Guardian*, and the paper was supplied with, among other things, the full text of the minutes of the meetings of EU Ministers for Social Welfare. These indicated what appeared to be sharp practice both by the EU and the British minister involved, in the way in which a directive on the rights of young workers was to operate. It appeared that the British were given an unpublished derogation, but there was concern that if the derogation were fully publicised the European Parliament would object. It seemed like a clear demonstration of the worth of freedom of information legislation. In fact the *Guardian* was so pleased that it sought further information, this time on immigration policy. On this occasion the minutes were withheld. These were confidential, they were told. And so also, they were told, were the minutes they had received previously: they had been released 'in error'. The Council of Ministers decided that they didn't really want to allow access by the media to 'confidential' records. What was a confidential record? A record the council didn't want to disclose, of course! According to the *Guardian*, only two countries—Denmark and the Netherlands—supported them. Ireland, apparently, remained silent. As I write, the *Guardian* is pursuing the matter through the European Court of Justice.

A similar attitude is to be seen in the excuses that are made to justify the domestic secrecy that was described earlier. In some cases the security of the state is invoked, in other cases it's the complexity of the issues. Information that is capable of being misunderstood is another great category, as is the possibility that some disclosures might 'discourage enterprise'. It is also interesting to note that the state, ironically, becomes so sensitive to personal privacy when it's asked to allow ordinary citizens access to its records. It appeared, by contrast, that Garda reports on the Emmet Stagg affair were available to large numbers of civil servants without any inhibiting concern for Mr Stagg's privacy.

And secrecy serves the purposes of national governments well when controversial EU policy decisions are taken at private meetings of the Council of Ministers following the submissions made by the Commission, which also meets in private. Ministers replace the rigours of domestic parliamentary scrutiny with a brief encounter with a harmless and relatively powerless European Parliament.

However, even though all this may lie under the surface, we are supposed to believe that we live in a functioning democracy. It is useful, therefore, to invoke the will or lack of will of the people as a first defence against subversive ideas on accountability. The first rebuttal of demands for change inevitably is that 'there's no demand for it.' Politicians and indeed senior civil servants will assure us that they are unaware of any widespread public demand for such changes. Some of them find it entertaining to invoke the imagery of the French Revolution to elaborate on this. They talk of their certainty that people are not going to 'take to the barricades' to demand freedom of information. And of course they are right. People, in an increasingly competitive world, have little enough time to pursue these matters. So we will try to help, remembering that the real reason for all the secrecy is not so much concern for the security of the state as concern arising out of the insecurity of the average politician and bureaucrat. This unstated reason for resistance was perhaps identified by the former Ombudsman, Michael Mills, when he explained to the Consumers' Association that his right of access to all documents on any case he was investigating was the bedrock of his powers. The Ombudsman is not alone in recognising that fact, and since the system obviously works at present to the advantage of the rulers, the mentality of 'if it's not broken don't fix it' prevails.

Any real revolution of openness will not come from the top. We may well get what amounts to a reluctant tokenism, with various protections and exceptions and at least one catch-all opting-out provision. To justify all this we will find all the reasons listed above trotted out. It would be possible to deal with all these objections in the abstract, but it is perhaps easier and definitely more entertaining to deal with these by reference to the experience of other countries, and particularly the United States. We can do that by looking at the key features of a real freedom of information culture and the minimum we need in Irish law.

16 A FREEDOM OF INFORMATION ACT

● ●

So what should be in a Freedom of Information Act? There are many models available, varying from the extremely detailed to the vaguely general. Sweden's Freedom of the Press Act, though containing only the most general of principles, has produced a culture of openness that has no parallel. In spite of all that, however, it did not expose scandals involving the bribery of potential customers of the very tightly regulated Swedish armaments industry. By contrast, the American act, passed originally in 1966, amended to make it work better in 1976, and amended slightly (after the Congress fought off Reagan's attempts to emasculate it) in the 1980s, is detailed and specific. The Australian act is even more detailed but less comprehensive.

The degree of detail is of course dependent both on a country's legal tradition and on the degree to which legislators believe that those implementing the legislation will operate according to its spirit. All this means, if my experience is anything to go by, that such legislation in Ireland will have to be as detailed as possible. The decision to make the fullest possible use of the exemptions and limitations in the EC Directive on Environmental Information and the range of protection the state gave itself in the Data Protection Act make this an unfortunate necessity. If they are not pinned down they will wriggle out of as much as possible. When we look later at the manner in which many US agencies have attempted to subvert their own act it will be even clearer why detail is needed. This means that the legislation will need to be clear and explicit about

(1) what records are covered and what records are exempt;

(2) what agencies are covered;

(3) who can look for information;

(4) what procedures are required to be followed by those seeking information;

(5) what time scale must be observed by the agency providing information;

(6) what charges can be made for the provision of information;

(7) what procedures are required for review of decisions to refuse access.

It is quite simple to sort out the records that are covered: either all records (other than those covered by specific exemptions) are covered or the reform is meaningless. All 'escape routes' will be willingly and imaginatively used. And of course records must be defined and prioritised.

Different kinds of records, depending on the extent of their importance and applicability, are assigned different priority. The American act begins by defining records that because of their importance and wide applicability must be published. This includes such things as an agency's organisational structures, procedures, rules and so on that are of 'general applicability'.

The next category of records is of those that must be made available 'for public inspection and copying' but are not formally published. These include 'final opinions, including concurring and dissenting opinions, as well as orders made in the adjudication of cases,' and also, among other things, 'administrative staff manuals and instructions to staff that affect a member of the public.'

Finally, all other non-exempt records must be made 'promptly available' when a request 'reasonably describes' such records. In all cases 'records' mean not just paper but electronic records too.

Which agencies are covered? In the United States all agencies are covered: this means agencies, offices and departments of the executive branch of the government. Specific examples include the Environmental Protection Agency, the Department of Defense, the State Department, the Tennessee Valley Authority (a development agency), and the Postal Service. In Ireland that would mean that all Government departments and commercial and non-commercial state and semi-state bodies would be covered.

While the act in the United States does not apply either to the Congress or to units within the president's office, it does apply to both the FBI and the CIA. This is especially interesting in the light of the Irish Government's decision to exempt all 'security-related' data from the provisions of the Data Protection Act. Obviously Irish Governments have bigger security worries than their American equivalents! Our big worry here would be the likelihood that the Government would refuse to provide a legislative definition of the agencies covered and instead rely on regulations to identify such agencies. This would naturally increase the likelihood that individual agencies would lobby the Government (in private, of course!) to be exempt rather than having to argue their case (in public) before a court.

The fact that an agency is covered by the provisions of a Freedom of Information Act doesn't mean that it is going to be obliged to disclose all, or indeed any, of its records. There are always exemptions to disclosure, and, as we saw when we looked at the Data Protection Act, Irish Governments love exemptions. So careful are Governments in fact that we are led to believe that it is the consideration of precise definition of these exemptions that has made progress in legislation on access to information so slow.

The duration of the deliberations and the significance attached to them bear with them at least two clear implications. The first is that we are entering new territory, where no precedents exist. The other is that even occasional disclosures of information that the Government didn't want disclosed would jeopardise one or other of the institutions of the state. The difficulty for defenders of these positions is of course that many of us know by now that neither is valid. American law and judicial decisions together have clarified the standard exemptions, and Irish Governments can hardly argue with any conviction that their situation is more complex than that of the US government. And Sweden has been dealing with these alleged complexities of definition for two hundred years or so. So no-one can seriously believe that difficulty of definition is the problem.

As far as the fear of accidental disclosure goes—and that possibility does exist, because no-one can forecast court interpretations of law—American experience would suggest that, however troublesome it may have been, no great institutions have fallen. My own suspicion is that either we are awaiting British legislation, out of which we can then steal convenient and (knowing Westminster) restrictive exemptions, or else we are not going to have such an act at all. (We might opt for the weak 'code of practice' that John Major introduced instead.) Another likely possibility is that, having observed the effectiveness of American and Swedish legislation, our leaders are trying to work out a way of giving us what they will call freedom of information while ensuring that they suffer none of the embarrassment that has from time to time resulted for their American counterparts. Saving face rather than secrecy may well be the problem.

So what records should be exempt? This is fairly well agreed by now, and we can go through them quite quickly provided we enter one caveat first. That is that there can be no blanket exemptions of the kind provided in the Data Protection Act, where non-disclosure would be assured simply by the opinion of a minister. Ministerial inclinations to suppress awkward information were well documented at the beef tribunal, and it would be a disaster if they were given yet another escape. They never refuse them! With that caveat, let us look at the American situation.

The first and obvious exemption must apply to records that need to be secret 'in the interests of national security or foreign policy.' This may sound reasonable but in practice it has been interpreted to exempt almost all the records held by the CIA and to give considerable protection to FBI records. Even this didn't satisfy the Reagan administration, which made huge, but unsuccessful, efforts to amend the act. The exemption of the FBI and CIA was assisted by presidential executive orders that gave the maximum possible latitude to the term 'state secret'. President Clinton has reduced the scope of such executive orders, and perhaps more CIA and FBI records will now become accessible.

Under the American act it's not ultimately up to the government to decide what is exempt or what is released: the final decision on these matters is taken by the courts. There is a large body of legal precedent in this area dealing with such genuinely complex matters as the government's right not to confirm or deny the existence of records where it could convince a court that this was the correct procedure, and also with the circumstances under which a court may insist on sight of a record before making a final decision. The courts, nevertheless, are supreme. Agencies can argue, sometimes successfully, that courts should not inspect records before making a decision, but it is the courts, not the government, that decide. This is not ideal, but we must recognise that the US government has got real secrets and also has a significant covert overseas operation. We, of course, have not, but we are still, as evidenced by the Data Protection Act, more protective of our records than the United States.

Whatever the reasons for our reticence, it can't just be national security. To suggest this would be to imply that the courts cannot be trusted to protect the institutions of the state. That is clearly both offensive and nonsensical. What courts *cannot* be relied upon to do is to protect the Government and its agencies from embarrassment or ridicule. For many this, not to mention cover-ups of activities of dubious legality, is sufficient reason for secrecy.

Another significant and potentially debilitating exemption applies to records that are 'specifically exempted from disclosure by statute.' As it stands, that could exempt all the records held by bodies such as the EPA, FÁS, Eolas, the HEA, etc. All of these have a catch-all 'confidentiality' clause in their statutory foundation. This gives the agency carte blanche to declare confidential anything it thinks appropriate. Governments would love an exemption in those terms. The American exemption is heavily qualified; indeed it says in effect that where an agency has discretion whether to disclose information or not, it cannot claim exemption, even if it has a legal right to declare some documents confidential. Only information that is specifically identified as being always and under all circumstances confidential can be held exempt. It appears that this was inserted in the American act more as a precautionary principle than as a general exemption, but it has resulted in a considerable judicial record that has interpreted confidentiality requirements and prohibition on disclosure quite narrowly. Nevertheless the qualification on the use of 'confidentiality' clauses in other legislation has been effective. It had to be inserted in 1976 because of what the Congress felt were excessively pro-secrecy interpretations of earlier legislation. Now the general principle can still be diluted by specific legislation, but not very much. A failure by Irish Governments to follow the American 1976 amendment could result in blanket exemptions being granted, either deliberately or accidentally, to most state agencies.

'Trade secrets and commercial or financial information obtained from a person and privileged and confidential' are also exempt. In principle this makes sense, but in practice it has proved contentious. A couple of things are clear, though. The first is that if information was generated by the government it cannot be covered by this exemption. The second is that a pledge of confidentiality by an agency will not qualify requested material as confidential under this section. It is interesting that this section has turned out to be among the most contentious, partly because commercial information has been among the most sought-after categories under the American act but also because of the number of occasions on which people who submitted information to an agency have sought to prevent its disclosure to a third party. Nevertheless the sense of the exemption has been found by the courts to mean that if disclosure could either impair the government's ability to obtain necessary information in the future or cause substantial harm to the competitive position of the person from whom the information was obtained, disclosure can be refused.

Not all American exemptions can be directly applied to Ireland. This would be the case with respect to exemption 5, which was inserted to preserve executive privilege as American judicial interpretations had defined it. It protects from disclosure any documents that would arguably not be accessible by way of a discovery motion in litigation. This protects, for instance, 'advice, recommendations, and opinions which are part of the deliberative, consultative, decision-making processes of government.' It also protects memorandums such as legal advice from lawyers to government agencies, and much more. It is a much-tested exemption that has resulted in a considerable amount of information, both factual and otherwise, being withheld. Complex legal issues have been involved. There has been much discussion, for instance, about the difference between the status of advice given before a decision is made and of advice after a decision is made. The detail can't be dealt with here, but the fear must be that, as always, Irish Governments would use the existence of a judicially constrained exemption like this to give themselves yet another blanket of cover.

Privacy is another matter that must be covered by exemption. The American act is careful to balance the right of privacy against the public interest. The exemption applies to 'personnel and medical files and similar files the disclosure of which would constitute a clearly unwarranted invasion of personal privacy.' Subsequent litigation has resulted in great emphasis being placed on the words 'clearly unwarranted'. There is no blanket guarantee of non-disclosure here: indeed the overwhelming weight of judicial decisions is that the exemption as written 'instructs the court to tilt the balance in favour of disclosure,' in so far as the disclosure of 'personal' information will shed light on the operations or activities of some government agency or official. And of course there is much more, one interesting decision being that the exemption is limited to individuals, and neither businesses nor business associations can claim exemption for reasons of personal privacy.

However, the most sweeping exemption, which will undoubtedly appeal to the Irish establishment, applies to records 'compiled for law enforcement purposes.' Interestingly, it is not necessarily to be assumed that all records compiled by law enforcement agencies are compiled for law enforcement purposes. This has to be proved in court. Where this is done, disclosure can be refused, but only to the extent that disclosure would result in one or more of a number of possible damaging consequences. These include damage to enforcement proceedings, interference with the right to a fair trial, invasion of privacy, disclosure of a confidential source, disclosure of investigative techniques, or endangering the life or physical safety of any person. And of course, as always, interpretations of all of these can be and are teased out in the courts. Contrast this yet again with the Data Protection Act, which gives absolute authority to the *opinion* of a minister.

The other American exemptions relate to oil-well data, representing, many believe, the strength of a particular lobby in the US Congress, and virtually all the records of 'an agency responsible for the regulation or supervision of financial institutions'—music to the ears of the Central Bank and the Department of Finance, no doubt!

But even if we were to get the relatively precise American exemptions, official agencies would have many other ways of frustrating our curiosity, not to mention our democracy. Among the most widely practised during the development of American legislation were the imposition of unreasonable charges, the incidence of enormous delays, and the demand for such precise information about records being sought that only someone who had the records in their possession could supply the details requested. This facilitated large-scale refusals.

Legislation will therefore have to circumscribe such evasions. We can be hopeful that seeking excessively detailed advance description will not be a problem here. The Department of the Environment has insisted that in the otherwise heavily flawed implementation of the EU Directive on Freedom of Information on the Environment, a reasonable description is all that is required. The others will still need to be dealt with. In particular, delay will have to be kept under control. There are agencies in the United States that can take years to provide requested information, even though the legislation specifies that they meet requests within a maximum of ten days, or twenty days in 'unusual circumstances'. Unfortunately the American courts have also ruled that where an agency is making reasonable efforts to meet requests they are meeting their legal obligations if requests are dealt with strictly in rotation; so ten days can stretch into years. Imagine what might happen in Ireland, where we have already picked two months as our target response time.

And then there are costs and fees. These can be used to intimidate if not frustrate seekers after information. An Irish regime that charges £7 for a copy of a planning decision could do wonders with large-scale requests for documents. Observation of the charges applied for the disclosure of information on the environment will enlighten us here, though the multiplicity of fees for participation in the planing process reveals a lot about the official mind! In the United States, charges have been used to deter many seekers after information. Indeed so widespread was the practice of imposing heavy fees that the Congress yet again amended the Freedom of Information Act in 1986 in an effort to reduce and standardise fees. Different fees are now allowed depending on the nature of the application for disclosure. For instance, when disclosure is sought for what are described as commercial interests the applicant can be charged not just the cost of copying but also the cost of time consumed in finding the requested records and also of 'reviewing them'—that is, the cost of the time consumed in deciding what parts of the records are to be withheld and what parts are to be disclosed. For non-commercial applications, only costs associated with copying the requested records can be charged. This usually means photocopying, or perhaps printing if computer records are involved. This fee regime applies to educational institutions, non-commercial research organisations, and the communications media. The act also makes provision for the complete waiver of fees, including even copying fees, where the disclosure is 'in the public interest'.

It's worth noting that these amendments were passed by the Congress but are implemented by the Office of Management and Budget. This office under Ronald Reagan managed to interpret what were meant to be facilitatory amendments with imaginative perversity. It appeared to many observers that their guidelines were designed to be as restrictive as possible and what's more to maximise the revenues of agencies from freedom of information work. President Reagan was no friend of the culture of freedom of information. Where he could he used executive orders to restrict access to information and made enormous efforts to have the act amended. The 1986 amendments were a compromise response to those efforts, which also facilitated both the CIA and the FBI. Both agencies had complained endlessly since the passage of the 1976 amendments that their work was being made impossible. They never really convinced the Congress, but President Reagan was more sympathetic.

Charges and bureaucratic delays aren't the only obstacle to access to information, of course. A simple and efficient procedure of appeals against refusal of disclosure must be in place. In the United States there is first of all a right of appeal to a higher agency authority. This must be availed of before any appeal can be made to the courts, which are the next level of appeal. The act instructs courts to give priority to freedom of information cases, but delays of two or three years are still possible. In spite of that many hundreds of such cases are held annually, almost all of them in Washington.

We can learn from the experience of the United States and simplify our procedures. In this regard I believe the bill I introduced in 1985 to be defective. This provided for appeal to the District Court in the event of refusal of disclosure, a procedure that is both cumbersome and costly for the applicant. It might not be too efficient either. On the other hand it appears that the Data Protection Commissioner, notwithstanding the flaws in the legislation, has done a remarkable job in ensuring that state and other agencies 'behave themselves'. The Ombudsman has been similarly successful, again with less than ideal legislative backing and indeed with Government hostility on occasion.

An Information Ombudsman established under a comprehensive Freedom of Information Act with an independent office and with adequate resources would save citizens the enormous cost of litigation except in the most exceptional circumstances—that is, provided he or she is not constricted by the sort of act that is passed by the Oireachtas. If ministers are given powers similar to those in the Data Protection Act then neither courts nor Ombudsman will be much use to us. Even if the legislation is perfect, the Information

Ombudsman won't be able to resolve every difficulty. Ultimately different interpretations of legislation or issues of conflicting rights have to be resolved by the courts and will end up there. But such an office could deal with huge numbers of administrative problems and indeed problems of detail as well. It would also with time ensure a reasonably uniform interpretation of legislation within and between agencies.

A lot more detail is required for such legislation to succeed. There would need to be clear procedures for the indexing of records, something that apparently doesn't happen at present. The state of the 'environmental records' made available by Cork County Council in 1993 adds weight to that view.

There is also the question of who would be entitled to make an application under a Freedom of Information Act. The provisions of the American act are available to anyone, not just to American citizens. It is possible therefore to seek from the US State Department information supplied by the US embassy in Dublin. I am now in the process of seeking such records from the State Department. In the past, at the height of the Cold War, the Soviet Union's TASS news agency regularly obtained information under the American act! With luck we'll be just as liberal. This might, for instance, enable people adjudged to be illegal immigrants to seek information in order to defend their case.

Finally, let us remember again that we are not suggesting radical innovation. We are merely attempting to have our democracy catch up with much of the rest of the world.

Other countries apart from the United States have introduced such legislation, though many have imposed substantial restrictions. The Australian act exempts a large number of federal agencies completely from its provisions. These include such bodies as the Aboriginal Land Councils and Land Trust and the Snowy Mountains Engineering Authority. As well as those blanket exemptions an even larger number of bodies have exemptions covering specified material. Programme material of the Australian Broadcasting Corporation is exempt, for instance! And then just to make doubly sure, some decisions to refuse disclosure are not open to any appeal if a minister so certifies.

New Zealand has a similar but broader ministerial power of certification.

Sweden's style of open government is the one most talked about in Europe, even though the legislative basis for freedom of information there is a good deal less comprehensive and precise than that in the United States or perhaps even in Australia. Sweden has, after all, a Secrecy Act. The freedom of information law is contained within the Freedom of the Press Act. Chapter 2 is entitled 'On the public character of official documents'. Article 1 begins: 'To further free interchange of opinions and enlightenment of the public ...' and goes on to set out the right to access to official documents. The range of bodies covered is extensive, including the obvious ones such as government departments but also (unlike the American act) including the parliament and, intriguingly, both the General Church Assembly and the Office of the Defence Command. All the bodies listed are required 'free of charge' to make official documents 'which are not to be kept secret ... available, immediately or as soon as possible, to any person who desires to have access to the document for the purpose of reading or copying it.' A charge can be made for copying documents.

Interestingly, the Swedish law also contains provisions that seem quite restrictive. It states in article 10: 'There shall be no right of appeal against any decision of the head of a ministry,' and in article 8 it is provided that a document need not be made available at the place where it is kept 'if that would meet with considerable difficulties.'

Swedish law seems not to differ much from that of other countries. Indeed the American law appears to be more generous, because of the universal right of appeal to the courts. And yet Sweden is in practice perhaps the most open country in the world, with journalists routinely examining departmental files and even the Prime Minister's correspondence. The *Guardian* published the text and a copy of a letter from the British Conservative MP Teresa Gorman to the Swedish Prime Minister warning him of the dangers of European federalism. Ms Gorman didn't expect to have her letter published, but Swedish practice ensured that it happened!

Other countries have freedom of information legislation too.

Most notable are Denmark, Norway, and Finland. France has also attempted to open up its official records, as has Canada.

Unfortunately the tide of information is not about to sweep across Europe. The EU's attitude to its own limited experiment with liberalisation in 1993 suggests no imminent breakthrough. The Irish Government's apparent indifference (and possibly agreement, but that might be confidential too!) and indeed the apparent lack of awareness of the controversy in the Irish media suggest that inertia is still firmly in place here.

Even more distressing is the fact that even a comprehensive or revolutionary Freedom of Information Act would only be the beginning of change. A much more dramatic institutional revolution is needed if we are to revitalise democracy and indeed return it to the idealistic vision it once represented.

17 ONLY THE BEGINNING

● ●

I t is perhaps an indicator of how passive we have all become, and indeed how overpowered we have been by the propaganda of the established order, that we would regard freedom of information as a revolution. It is no more than the beginnings of change.

Freedom of information would give us the right to know a good deal about what the state and its institutions know. That would be progress, but we would still be very much the servants of the institutions, not their masters. Huge parts of the state's power are exercised not by Government departments or by local authorities but by semi-state agencies of various kinds. These range from unobtrusive bodies like the National Drugs Advisory Board, doing an important job in the background to protect us from the short-cuts of greedy multinationals, to FÁS, a massive organisation with a logo visible in every parish and with control of a budget in the region of £100 million. Freedom of information would give us some access to the records of these agencies, and that would be progress indeed.

But it would be information after the event. We would know what information was used as a basis for decision-making; we would have access to information the agency had that it used to assess its own performance; and we would have access to the criteria it claimed to use in the award of contracts and the expenditure of public money. But we would not know how the agency reached a decision. Nor would we have any access to details of informal contacts between an agency and the various bodies it deals with. The submissions many of these agencies make to the Government are often confidential, and of course their boards never meet in public. Most of these bodies are in effect organised as if they were private agencies. They report to the Government, of course, but are at best indirectly accountable to the Oireachtas.

The problem clearly is that while many of the records of such bodies would be immediately available to us as soon as we were aware of their existence, we won't actually become aware of that until they have made a decision. The solution is to change the law. There is clearly no sense in bodies meeting in private to discuss matters that are covered by a Freedom of Information Act. They should meet in public, except when matters that are clearly exempt from public disclosure are being discussed. Why should the board of FÁS meet in private when it is deciding to whom it should award a contract or when it is discussing its future strategy? Why should it meet in private to decide on its response to various aspects of Government policy? Why should the public be denied the right to know how members of such boards vote on controversial issues? Why should their minutes be confidential?

The problem is not confined to huge agencies like FÁS. It crops up at local level too. Indeed secrecy has increased as a result of changes, particularly in the educational field, or at least in the area of vocational education. Vocational educational committees meet in public, at least some of the time, and when they were directly responsible for the schools and colleges in their area, that gave some small level of transparency, even if every 'difficult' decision was taken in private. The advent of boards of management and more recently the granting of autonomy to the RTCs has changed all that. Boards of management and governing bodies of RTCs meet always in private, and there is no provision for them to do otherwise. VECs used to discuss at least the broad outline of RTC policy in public, and that is no more. Why should such boards and bodies meet in private?

Obsessive privacy is not a monopoly of semi-state organisations. Local authorities and health boards seem to find secrecy convenient too, and indeed can often decide to meet 'in camera' without, as we've seen, any clear criteria for doing so. Only the Oireachtas is governed by a fairly all-embracing injunction to openness, an injunction that does not extend to its committees—or at least not to the committees I have been a member of. It appeared to me that much of the most interesting business of such committees was always discussed in private. I remember a meeting of the Joint Committee on Building Land at which a member of An Bord Pleanála gave a less than flattering account of the work practices of members of the board. It would have made a great story, but we were told it all in private!

So we go on. The Arts Council, Forbairt, the NCEA, the HEA, Shannon Development, the National Roads Authority, the Competition Authority, the IRTC, the RTE Authority, Comhairle na nOspidéal, the EPA and Údarás na Gaeltachta, to name but a few, control between them hundreds of millions of pounds, mostly provided by the taxpayer, and are in the position to make decisions that can allocate or regulate control of other equally valuable public resources, like the quality of our air and water. They belong to us, and yet they are obliged to give us no more than the end-of-year figures and bland generalisations that characterise their annual reports. They neither look nor, apparently, feel accountable. A breach in the wall of secrecy would change all that. And if the spirit of freedom of information really took hold they would have nothing left to hide.

That is precisely why the Open Government ('Government in the Sunshine') Act was passed in the United States in 1976. It says that, subject to exemptions, most of which are broadly similar to those in the Freedom of Information Act, 'every portion of every meeting of an agency shall be open to public observation.' There are extra exemptions, but these are quite narrowly based and sensible. They deal with the need to allow the agency to litigate without having to make premature disclosure of its views and similar matters and with the need for it to be able to come to decisions and take actions where premature disclosure could harm its work. The exemptions specifically do not cover decisions about budgetary matters, including cuts in expenditure, nor can they be used to 'shelter the substandard performance of government executives.'

The act is obviously intended to be much more than a token gesture. It goes into some detail to define a 'meeting' so as to ensure that public meetings are not just ritual rubber-stamping exercises, with real decisions having been taken earlier. The real decisions must be taken at the real meetings. Even a telephone conference involving a quorum of the members of the body is identified as a meeting and cannot take decisions. There is a large section prohibiting 'ex-parte' communications (communications between the agency and other bodies or individuals that are not recorded and made available as part of the records of the agency). Consequently all communications between the agency and any interested body must be matters of record.

All this would be a shock both to our bureaucracy and to all those members of the party faithful who are nominated to various state bodies. They would have to make all their records public, hold most of their meetings in public, and make their views known. And they would not be allowed to have any of the cosy private meetings with friends or allies that are so much a part of Irish political culture. Possession of a position would be a poor protection. We would begin to be able to adjudicate on performance!

These reforms can't just apply to statutory bodies providing services to the public. There can be no justifiable reason why bodies like the National Economic and Social Council, the National Economic and Social Forum, the National Monuments Advisory Board and the myriad of other advisory bodies should go on their merry private way. How do they form their conclusions? Does the Government affect their thinking, or even the thinking of individual members? How do trade union representatives vote on the NESC? Do they all read those reports? What sort of responses do they make? If we knew all that we'd begin to feel we were in control again!

Our demand for reform must go further, however. There can be no tolerance for the sad and timid Data Protection Act that was foisted on us. That act must be extended and amended. It must be extended to guarantee both the right to privacy of and the right of access to all personal files, whether on computer or not. If they have them and they can use them, we should have the right to see them and correct them. And this is particularly true if the files are in the possession of the Gardaí or intelligence service. They can have no right to keep false information on anyone, nor to disclose it as they see fit, for whatever purpose they deem appropriate.

The urge to reform cannot be confined to the public sector. We cannot make churches more democratic, but we can make the agencies they control more accountable by extending legislation on information and open meetings to them. We can make the various committees meet in public, and make their records accessible. We can do the same for private business, by first of all bringing our disclosure laws into line with those in other countries. The benefits and privileges of limited liability should only be available to those who are prepared to be identified and accountable under law. Similarly those who raise money from the public as public limited companies must be required to tell us all that a properly functioning market economy needs. And we could go from there to initiate demands for a social and an environmental audit from all such companies. We might even demand that they tell their employees the full story about the company's performance.

Of course this is revolutionary. It would be nothing less than a transformation of the political and business culture of the country. It would restore a sense of popular control over the state and its institutions and would probably do wonders to dilute the almost universal cynicism that has infected public attitudes to politics. It might even get the media interested in news again!

And it works. All over the United States public bodies meet in public, with pre-publicised agenda and all the documents available to the press and to the public, and all discussions with individuals placed on the record. Contrary to expectations, this doesn't produce long speeches by publicity-seekers, nor does it inhibit people from expressing their views. It does, however, reduce the possibility of shady or sloppy dealing. It makes rational decision-making more likely and reminds all agencies that they are in the service of and accountable to the people, not just the government. And the courts are there to make sure they don't forget.

Why not do it in Ireland? As usual, the objections that will be raised will not be directly negative. Everybody will agree in principle. 'Practicalities' will be raised. But by now we can see that these are no more than a smoke-screen. The real fear is the fear of accountability—the fear of democracy. There can be no complexity, no secrets, no commercial information in the hands of any Irish agency that is not replicated a thousandfold in the United States. And the heavens don't fall! Our problem is indeed the practicalities, but not the practicalities of reform. What causes concern in Ireland are not the uncertainties of accountability but the certainties, in particular the certainty of exposure of the underlying culture of quasi-corruption that now taints so much of our public life.

We have tried the route of one-dimensional economics, and while it may have made us richer it manifestly didn't make us much better off. We are now faced with a further set of demands from the radical right, to go even further down their one-dimensional cul-de-sac. This route has led to declining services, collapsing infrastructure and social inequality where it has been tried. We could try something different. We could try institutional revolution. We could restore democratic accountability and thus public participation. And we would make all those who are responsible defend the quality of our services.

Many would be inconvenienced by all this. Indeed the trade unions might not like it; but it would make a wonderful manifesto for a genuine movement of the left. Nothing is more left-wing than democracy. Let us have more of it, and quickly!

Postscript

● ●

This book was written as the events of 1994 unfolded and the public mood and the political mood shifted more and more in the direction of 'accountability' and 'transparency'. We got the commitment to introduce a Freedom of Information Act and an aspiration to make public bodies transparent. But a lot was left out.

There has been no commitment to amend the Data Protection Act, despite repeated criticisms from the Data Commissioner. The increasing public demand for a widening of the Ombudsman's brief has so far found no response, and the Health and Safety Authority is unable to tell us if its report on a serious accident in a factory in Cork will ever be made public. Will we ever know the criteria by which 'investment' can be rewarded with an Irish passport? Most of us would feel that if an individual wants an Irish passport then the Irish people ought to know what exactly their contribution to our well-being is going to be.

More distressing still though is the apparent absence of a commitment to institutional reform to go hand in hand with the information reform. The furtive secrecy of all state agencies is apparently accepted. Company law reform is not on the agenda at all, and we haven't even mentioned accountability in the trade union movement.

A great opportunity will be missed. Just for once there is a political focus on how democracy works. The outcome of that focus will be one of two things. Either we will have reform that will reinvigorate all of us by transferring power back to individuals and communities, or we will have a law that does no more than enable us to look at the records of our institutional failure. The short-cut would be easy, but the revolution is what we need. Are there any revolutionaries in government?

INDEX

abortion, 10, 29–30
Adams, Gerry, 11
Ahern, Bertie, 77, 114
AIDS, 24, 33
air pollution, 40, 45
Allied Irish Banks, 90
Angola, 147
Army intelligence, 55
arrest, unlawful, 52–4
Arts Council, The, 178
Association of Higher Civil
    Servants, 154
Atlantic 252, 39
ATMs, 106
Augustinian survey, 139
Australia, 163, 173

Bank of Ireland, 90
banking, 89–91, 93, 106–7, 133–4,
    149
  data trading, 97
  and environment, 136–7
  legislation, 7
bankruptcy, 134–5
beef tribunal, 84, 166
Bermingham, George, 73
Best, Keith, 33–4
Birmingham Six, 73
boards of management, 14–15, 120
  getting information from, 127–9
bond-washing, 91
Bord Fáilte, 30, 131
Bord Pleanála, An, 38–9, 40, 41,
    46, 47, 77, 178
  judicial function, 45

Bowman, John, 8
Brennan, Seamus, 77
Britain, 57, 60, 137, 139
  data protection, 93
  freedom of information, 155, 166
  media, 146–7
  security, 56
  social welfare derogation, 160
Broadcasting Act (Section 31),
    10–11
Bruton, John, 156
Building Land, Joint Committee
    on, 178
building societies, 2, 7, 75, 87–90,
    103
Business Age, 86

Cambodia, 147
Campaign for Nuclear
    Disarmament (CND), 51–2, 104
Canada, 175
car registration, central, 102
Casey, Barney, 50
Casey, Éamonn, Bishop of
    Galway, 28
Castro, Fidel, 73
Catholic Church, 3, 9
  and boards of management,
    14–15
  church attendance, 150–51
  getting information from,
    139–41
  medical ethics, 28
  school patrons, 13, 127–8
censorship, 9–10, 143, 146
census data, 105–6

Center for National Security Studies, 138
Central Bank, 89–90, 133–4, 170
Central Intelligence Agency (CIA), 165, 166, 172
Central Statistics Office, 106
charities, 133
Child Care Act, 33
Children's Act, 150
China, 57
Chomsky, Noam, 147
Church of Ireland, 13
Citizens' Advice Bureaus, 72
civil service
    accountability, 15
    'flying file', 92
    and local authorities, 126–7
    obstructionism, 73
    and Oireachtas committees, 110
    secrecy, 33, 76–7, 161–2
Clare, Dr Anthony, 150–51
Clinical Trials Bill, 150
Clinton, Bill, 166
clothing allowances, 69
cohabitation, 60
Collins, Gerry, 74, 94
Comhairle na nOspidéal, 178
commercial information, 168
community information, 120–30
community schools, 128
Community Welfare Officer, 69
companies, 7–8, 83–5, 180. *see also* private sector
    AGMs, 2–3, 87, 90, 135–6
    flotation information, 135
    lack of disclosure, 86–7
    limited liability, 132–3
    ownership of, 129
    phoenix syndrome, 85
    safety standards, 130
Companies Office, 132, 133
company directors, 7, 83–4, 86–7
    fees, 83, 89
    liability of, 133
    non-executive, 88, 137
company law, 7, 84–6, 182
Competition Authority, The, 178
Comptroller and Auditor-General, 15, 23
computers, 92–3, 106–7, 138–9
    fraud, 106–7
Conference of Religious of Ireland, 20
confidentiality, 167–8
Conservative Party, 146
Constitution of Ireland, 17, 57, 79, 152, 157
Consumer Affairs, Director of, 75, 81
Consumer Choice, 135
consumer protection, 7–8, 80–91, 135
Consumers' Association, 81, 138, 154, 162
contraception, 10, 28–9
Control of Clinical Trials Act, 26
Coolock Community Law Centre, 64
Cork, 19, 182
    task force report, 76
Cork City Council, 38, 41
Cork County Council, 2, 173
Cork Harbour, 40
Cork RTC, 2, 23
corporate sector. *see* companies
Council of Europe, 93–4, 107
Council of Ministers, 160–61
counselling, 24
county managers, 123
covenanting, 19
credit institutions, 106–7
creditworthiness, 87–8, 93, 103
crime prevention, 169–70
    data protection, 96–7
Criminal Justice Bill, 51
Crowley, Niall, 90

Cuba, 72–3
cucumber poisoning, 6–7, 75
Curragh camp, 50
currency speculation, 136
Customs and Excise, 55

Dáil Éireann. *see* Oireachtas
data, sources of, 102–8
Data Protection Act, 88, 94–101,
    102, 104, 105, 107
  data trading, 97–9
  exemptions and limitations,
    163, 165, 166, 167
  finance, 96
  need for extension, 179–80, 182
  opinion of minister, 170
  paper records, 26, 99–101
  personal data, 96–9
  security, 94–6
  student assessments, 23
Data Protection Commissioner,
    98–100, 103, 172, 182
de Valera, Eamon, 8
Defence, Department of, 55, 104,
    108
  data protection, 94–5, 96
Defence Forces, 54, 95, 96, 106
  review of, 76
democracy
  defence of, 6–7
  emergency legislation, 49–50
  fear of, 181
  and freedom of information,
    157–62
democratic deficit, 159–61
Denmark, 47, 161, 175
Desmond, Barry, 28
Desmond, Dermot, 84
dilation and curettage, 29–30
disability benefit, 66
District Court, 172
divorce referendum, 152
Doherty, Seán, 71, 95

drug companies, 26–7
Dublin City Council, 46, 100, 122,
    125
Dublin County Council, 46
Dukes, Alan, 91

E numbers, 82
Earthwatch, 45, 46
East Timor, 152
Eastern Health Board, 31
  economic policy, 4–5, 63, 181
  and institutional reform, 157–8
  and media, 148–50
ectopic pregnancy, 29
education, 12, 13–23, 158
  data protection, 98–9
  finance, 17–18, 19
  getting information, 127–9
  primary, 13–18, 127–8
  secondary, 18–20, 127, 128–9
  standards, 17
  third-level, 20–23
Education, Department of, 13–23,
    77, 102, 128
  accountability, 15
  and archives, 23
  identity numbers, 99, 103
  inspectorate, 17
  and Irish-language schools, 16
  and multidenominational
    schools, 16–17
effluent control, 42
El Salvador, 147
Electricity Supply Board (ESB),
    46, 69, 98, 102–3
emergency legislation, 49–50
emigration, 4
employers, 100
ENFO, 36
environment, 2, 7, 12, 35–47, 130
  and financial institutions, 136–7
  and industrial development,
    42–4

information on, 75–6, 123
licence applications, 40–41
and media, 151
and planning authorities, 36–40
Environment, Department of the,
36, 45, 69, 126, 134, 170
Environmental Information, EU
Directive on, 35, 156, 160
exemptions and limitations, 163
flaws, 12, 43–7, 170
Environmental Protection Agency
(EPA), 40–41, 167, 178
secrecy of, 43–5
Eolaire an Stáit, 111
Eolas, 22, 81, 167
ethics committees, 27–8, 30
European Convention on Human
Rights, 50
European Court of Justice, 161
European Parliament, 160, 161
European Union, 56, 81
company law, 86, 133
data protection, 93, 101
democratic deficit, 159–61
disclosure regulations, 109
freedom of information in,
160–61, 175
research applications, 22
Evening Herald, 107, 122
exchange controls, 7
executive privilege, 168

Factory Inspectorate, 77
Fair Trade Tribunal, 84
Family Planning Bill, 143
Farrell, Edmund, 88
FÁS, 78, 127, 167, 176, 177
Federal Bureau of Investigation
(FBI), 165, 166, 172
fees, 38, 171
Fianna Fáil, 1, 149, 151
Finance, Department of, 75, 89,
91, 111, 170

Finance Acts, 84
financial institutions, 3, 133–4, 170
data protection, 96
Financial Times, 135
Fine Gael, 52, 121, 154
Finland, 175
fisheries, 76
FitzGerald, Garret, 52, 121
Flynn, Pádraig, 110–11
food, safety of, 82
Football Association of Ireland
(FAI), 151
Forbairt, 22, 178
Foreign Affairs, Department of,
72–3, 102, 104
France, 56, 175
free market. *see* market economy
Freedom of Access to
Information, EU Declaration
on, 160
Freedom of Information Act
accidental disclosure, 166–9
as beginning, 176–81
difficulties of definition, 165–6
evasions, 170–72
fees, 171
plan for, 163–75
promise of, 156
right of appeal, 172–3
Freedom of Information Act (US),
23, 43, 138, 155, 158–9, 162,
163
agencies covered, 164–5
bureaucratic delays, 170–72
definition of records, 164
exemptions, 166–9
and government agencies, 55–6
right of application, 138, 173
Freedom of Information Bill,
1988, 71–2, 143–4, 154, 172

Gaelic Athletic Association
(GAA), 120, 151

Galway, 28
Garda Complaints Board, 53
Garda Síochána, 44, 102, 106, 148
    data protection, 95–6
    intelligence files, 180
    powers of, 49, 50–54
    records of, 55–6
    Stagg affair, 161
    and travellers, 61, 62
General Medical Service (GMS),
    30
Germany, 137
Goodman, Larry, 84, 129
Gorman, Teresa, 174
Government
    and EPA confidentiality, 43–4
    and freedom of information,
    156–62
    influence of, 116–17
    and local authorities, 41
    and media, 150, 152–3
    secrecy of, 6–7, 76–7
Green movement, 48
Greenpeace, 138
Gregory, Tony, 65
Guardian, 160–61, 174
Guatemala, 147
guide dogs, 125

hacking, 106–7
halting sites, 124–5
Hanrahan case, 43
Harvard Business Review, 73
Haughey, Charles, 94
Health, Department of, 26, 33,
    127
health, risks to, 82
Health and Safety at Work Act,
    130
Health and Safety Authority, 182
health boards, 28, 30, 102, 103,
    104, 116, 150, 178

getting information from, 126–7
    nursing home inspections,
    30–31
    secrecy of, 32–3
Health Education Bureau, 33
Health Promotion Unit, 33
health services, 5, 12, 24–34, 158
    cut-backs, 30
    ethics committees, 27–8, 30
    private patients, 30
    reproduction and sexuality,
    27–30
'hedging', 136
Higgins, Michael D., 53, 95
High Court, 39, 68, 135, 137
Higher Education Authority
    (HEA), 20–21, 167, 178
holistic care, 24
Homeless Persons Bill, 143
homelessness, 31, 61, 69
hospice movement, 24
Hot Press, 148
housing, 83, 121–2, 123–4
hunger-strike campaign, 52

immigration, 57–8, 160
industrial accidents, 77
industrial development, 42–4
Industrial Development Authority
    (IDA), 118, 127, 131, 138
Industry and Commerce,
    Department of, 84
Information Ombudsman, 172–3
insider trading, 85–6
Institute of Industrial Research
    and Standards (IIRS), 22–3
Institute of Public Administration
    (IPA), 111
interest rates, 149
International Financial Services
    Centre (IFSC), 94
International Monetary Fund
    (IMF), 146

Internet, 139
IPA Yearbook and Diary, 111
Irish, Joint Committee on, 74
Irish Congress of Trade Unions (ICTU), 4, 138, 141
Irish Council for Civil Liberties, 154
Irish Hospital Consultants' Association, 32
Irish Housewives' Association, 49, 104
Irish-language schools, 15–16
Irish Medical Council, 68, 115
Irish Medical Times, 31
Irish Permanent Building Society, 88–9, 90, 135
Irish Republican Army (IRA), 10, 50, 51, 57
Irish Times, 88, 144–5
IRTC, 178
Italy, 6

Jobsearch, 64
Justice, Department of, 33, 53–4, 74, 102, 108, 111
  data protection, 93, 94–5
  immigration, 57–8
  powers of, 53
  secrecy of, 51, 104
  security information, 55–6

Kelly, Nicky, 55
Kenny, Ivor, 143
Khmer Rouge, 147
Kiberd, Damien, 143

Labour, Department of, 77
Labour Party, 1, 121, 146, 154
Labour Party, British, 146
Land Registry, 134
landlord registration, 134
language, use of, 145–7
law and order. *see* security

law enforcement records, 169–70
Lee, River, 76
legal system, 39–40
  costs, 55
  and freedom of information, 167–70
letter interception, 53
libel, 132, 143, 158
Limerick, 18, 128
limited liability, 132–3
Livingstone, Ken, 146
lobbying, 109–10
local authorities, 102, 116, 134, 146, 178
  attendance at meetings, 122–3
  and environment, 36–40, 75–6
  expenses, 122
  getting information from, 121–7
  licence applications, 40–41
  refusal of information, 46–7
  'reserved' functions, 123
Lynch, Jack, 63
Lyons, F.S.L., 8

Maastricht referendum, 152
McCreevy, Charlie, 62
MacGowan, Shane, 29
McKenna, Patricia, 152
Macmillan, Harold, 79–80
McVerry, Fr Peter, 31
Major, John, 166
Marine, Department of the, 77
market economy, 5, 8, 79–91, 134
  banking, 90–91
  building societies, 87–90
  company law, 83–7
  food safety, 82
Martin, Michael, 41
means tests, 63, 104
Meath, County, 39
media, 4, 48, 143–53
  'colour' pieces, 147–8
  cynicism, 148–50

media *continued*
  and economics, 148–50, 158
  and propaganda, 152–3
  property supplements, 145, 151
  and Section 31, 10–12
  use of information, 129
  use of language, 145–7
medical cards, 30
medical certificates, 67–9, 115
medical ethics, 26–8
medical records, 25–6
Merck, Sharp and Dohme, 43
Mills, Michael, 162
Mother and Child scheme, 9
Mountjoy Jail, 57
Mozambique, 147
multidenominational schools, 14, 16–17
multinationals, 109, 137, 176

National Archives, 2, 23, 144
National Archives Advisory Committee, 23
National Council for Educational Awards (NCEA), 178
National Drugs Advisory Board, 176
National Economic and Social Council (NESC), 179
National Economic and Social Forum, 179
National Monuments Advisory Board, 179
National Roads Authority, 178
National Social Services Board, 72
Netherlands, the, 161
New Zealand, 56, 174
news agencies, 145
Nicaragua, 11, 147
Noonan, Michael, 51
North-Western Health Board, 31
Northern Ireland, 10–12, 145, 148
Norway, 175

nursing homes, 30–31, 33

O'Connell, Daniel, 8
O'Connell, Dr John, 25, 74
Offences Against the State Act, 50–52, 56–7
Office of Management and Budget, 171–2
Office of Public Works, 13
Official Secrets Act, 9, 143
oil-well data, 170
Oireachtas, houses of the, 96, 129
  accountability to, 177
  committee stage of bills, 115–16
  committees, 15, 74–5, 110, 178
  and freedom of information, 156–7
  law and order debate, 51
  media interest, 143–4, 149–50
  questions in, 92, 114–16, 131–2
  secrecy in, 73–5
Ombudsman, 46, 162, 172, 182
  for credit institutions, 106–7
O'Neill, Tip, 120
Open Government Act (US), 178–9
O'Reilly, Emily, 148

parish councils, 120
Parnell, C.S., 8
passports, 1, 182
pastoral care, 24
Patients' Charter, 25–6, 33
pensioners, 59, 60
Pentagon, 22–3
pharmaceutical industry, 26–7
phone tapping, 53–4, 71
Pilger, John, 147
planning authorities
  and environment, 36–40, 46–7
  and industrial development, 42–4
  and pollution, 45–6

Planning for the Future, 32
political parties, 112, 137
politicians, 6, 8–9
  getting information from,
    112–14, 117–18, 126–7, 128
  independent, 121–2
  and pressure, 117–18
pollution control licences, 40–41
Post, An, 98, 102, 104–5
poverty, 59–70
pressure groups, 109–10
primary education, 13–18
  free, 17–18
  getting information, 127–8
prison planning, 74
privacy, 169
private sector, 84. *see also*
  companies
  getting information from,
    131–42
  performance evaluation, 132
Procedures and Privileges
  Committee, 74
product evaluation, 81, 135
property ownership, 134
protests, public, 53–4
psychiatric care, 24, 32
Public Accounts Committee, 15
Public Expenditure Committee,
  74
public limited companies, 135–7,
  180
public safety, 6–7
public sector, 61, 114, 121, 147
  getting information from,
    109–11
  obsessive privacy, 178

quangos, 78
questionnaires, 98, 105

racial discrimination, 57–8
Radio Tara, 39

Rainbow Warrior, 56
rape, 29–30
Rapple, Colm, 149
ratepayers, 134
Reagan, Ronald, 11, 48, 49, 52,
  147, 149
restrictions on information, 55–6,
  155, 166, 171–2
records
  definition of, 164
  indexing of, 155, 173
  on paper, 26, 99–101
referendums, 51, 152
religious instruction, 18
residential property tax, 144–5
Revenue Commissioners, 55, 83,
  86, 102, 103–4, 114
  annual report, 111
Reynolds, Albert, 41, 79
rezoning, 123
Robinson, Mary, 71–2, 143
Ross, Shane, 85
RTCs, 21, 23, 177
RTE, 118, 152
  Section 31, 10–12
RTE Authority, 178
Rulings of the Chair, 73
Russia, 145–6, 173
Ryan, Louden, 90

safety at work, 130
St Vincent de Paul Society, 120
school transport, 77
Scoil an tSeachtar Laoch, 16
Seanad Éireann. *see* Oireachtas
search fees, 38, 171
secondary education, 18–20, 127,
  128–9
  appointments, 20
  private sector, 18–19
  streaming, 19
Section 4 motions, 41, 123

security, 48–58, 71, 74, 93, 161, 167
    asylum-seekers, 57–8
    computers, 106–7
    data protection, 94–6
    emergency legislation, 49–50
    judicial guidelines, 55
    legal expenses, 55
    Offences Against the State Act, 50–53
Security Committee, 55
semi-state bodies, 2, 78, 104–6, 117–19, 177–8
Shannon Development, 178
share options, 137
Shipley College, Bradford, 57
sick benefit, 66–9
Simon Community, 19
Single European Act, 152
single parents, 59–60
Sinn Féin, 10–12
small businesses, 86, 109, 133
Smith, Adam, 8
Smurfit Corporation, 43
Social Welfare, Department of, 72, 92, 102, 103, 104, 115, 134
    annual report, 111
    and data protection, 98–9
    fraud, 68, 75
    investigation unit, 60–62, 66
    medical referee, 67–8
    Supplementary Welfare Scheme, 69
    and travellers, 61–2
    and unemployed, 62–6
Social Welfare, EU Ministers of, 160–61
Social Welfare Act, 1993, 63
South Africa, 11, 137–8
South Tipperary County Council, 43
Southern Health Board, 32–3
sports, 151

Stagg, Emmet, 161
state bodies, 78, 100–101
State directory, 111
State-Sponsored Bodies, Committee on, 118–19
Status of Children Bill, 150
sterilisation, 27–9
Stock Exchange, 83, 84, 85–6, 135
Stubbs Gazette, 134–5
Sunday Business Post, 86, 143
Sunday Independent, 148
'sunshine act', 178–9
Supplementary Welfare Scheme, 69
Supreme Court, 10–12, 39, 55
Sweden, 158–9, 165
    Freedom of the Press Act, 163, 174

Tablet, 15, 140
Targetpoint, 98, 105
TASS news agency, 173
taxation, 1, 7, 83, 149
teachers, 14, 15, 20
Telecom Éireann, 84, 97–8, 102, 107
telephone interception, 53–4, 71
terrorism, 49, 51, 147
Thatcher, Margaret, 49, 146–7, 149, 155
tourism, 131
trade secrets, 168
trade unions, 91, 100, 114, 179, 182
    getting information from, 135, 139, 141–2, 181
    safety standards, 130
    secrecy in, 3–4
trades councils, 141
travellers, 61, 100
    and local authorities, 124–5
Treacy, Noel, 154
tubal ligation, 27

Udarás na Gaeltachta, 131, 178
unemployment, 4, 62–6
  benefits, 63
  and media, 150
United States, 3, 8, 47, 60, 139,
    180–81. *see also* Freedom of
    Information Act (US)
  and Cuba, 72–3
  data protection, 93
  Defense Department, 22–3
  disclosure rules, 86–7
  environment, 136–7
  EPA, 43
  health care, 5
  shareholder pressure, 137–8
  'sunshine act', 178–9
universities, 20–23
  corporate sponsorship, 21–2
  data protection, 98–9
  research, 21–3
  senators, 113

VECs, 116, 177
violence, renunciation of, 11–12
Vocational Education Acts, 18
voluntary groups, 69–70, 133

Walsh, Dr James, 33
water pollution, 40, 75–6, 110–11
weapons purchases, 55–6
welfare services, 59–70, 114, 158
  appeals, 65–6, 69
  cohabitation, 60
  fraud report, 75
  and media, 150
  sick benefit, 66–9
  and travellers, 61–2
  and unemployed, 62–6
Western Health Board, 31
Wexford, County, 40
Which, 135
Wicklow People, 1
Wicklow Urban District Council,
    1
widows' pensions, 60
women, rights of, 9–10
Woods, Michael, 60, 62, 65, 75
World Bank, 146

Yamanouchi plant, 46

Zhirinovski, 146